Edexcel GCSE (9-1)
History

Early Elizabethan England, 1558–1588

Series Editor: Angela Leonard   Author: Georgina Blair

ALWAYS LEARNING

PEARSON

Published by Pearson Education Limited, 80 Strand, London, WC2R 0RL.

www.pearsonschoolsandfecolleges.co.uk

Copies of official specifications for all Edexcel qualifications may be found on the website: www.edexcel.com

Text © Pearson Education Limited 2016

Series editor: Angela Leonard
Designed by Colin Tilley Loughrey, Pearson Education Limited
Typeset by Phoenix Photosetting, Chatham, Kent
Original illustrations © Pearson Education Limited
Illustrated by KJA Artists Illustration Agency and Phoenix Photosetting, Chatham, Kent.

Cover design by Colin Tilley Loughrey
Picture research by Christine Martin
Cover photo © Bridgeman Art Library Ltd: National Portrait Gallery, London, UK

The right of Georgina Blair to be identified as author of this work has been asserted by her in accordance with the Copyright, Designs and Patents Act 1988.

First published 2016

19 18 17
10 9 8 7

British Library Cataloguing in Publication Data
A catalogue record for this book is available from the British Library.
ISBN 978 1 292 12726 2

Printed in Slovakia by Neografia

A note from the publisher
In order to ensure that this resource offers high-quality support for the associated Pearson qualification, it has been through a review process by the awarding body. This process confirms that this resource fully covers the teaching and learning content of the specification or part of a specification at which it is aimed. It also confirms that it demonstrates an appropriate balance between the development of subject skills, knowledge and understanding, in addition to preparation for assessment.

Endorsement does not cover any guidance on assessment activities or processes (e.g. practice questions or advice on how to answer assessment questions), included in the resource nor does it prescribe any particular approach to the teaching or delivery of a related course.

While the publishers have made every attempt to ensure that advice on the qualification and its assessment is accurate, the official specification and associated assessment guidance materials are the only authoritative source of information and should always be referred to for definitive guidance.

Pearson examiners have not contributed to any sections in this resource relevant to examination papers for which they have responsibility.

Examiners will not use endorsed resources as a source of material for any assessment set by Pearson.

Endorsement of a resource does not mean that the resource is required to achieve this Pearson qualification, nor does it mean that it is the only suitable material available to support the qualification, and any resource lists produced by the awarding body shall include this and other appropriate resources.

Websites
Pearson Education Limited is not responsible for the content of any external internet sites. It is essential for tutors to preview each website before using it in class so as to ensure that the URL is still accurate, relevant and appropriate. We suggest that tutors bookmark useful websites and consider enabling students to access them through the school/college intranet.

Contents

Timeline   6

Chapter 1 Queen, government and religion, 1558–69   8

1.1 The situation on Elizabeth's accession   9

1.2 The 'settlement' of religion   18

1.3 Challenge to the religious settlement   26

1.4 The problem of Mary, Queen of Scots   32

Recap page   37

Writing Historically   38

Chapter 2 Challenges to Elizabeth at home and abroad, 1569–88   40

2.1 Plots and revolts at home   41

2.2 Relations with Spain   50

2.3 Outbreak of war with Spain, 1585–88   59

2.4 The Armada   61

Recap page   65

Writing Historically   66

Chapter 3 Elizabethan society in the Age of Exploration, 1558–88   68

3.1 Education and leisure   69

3.2 The problem of the poor   77

3.3 Exploration and voyages of discovery   84

3.4 Raleigh and Virginia   91

Recap page   99

Writing Historically   100

Early Elizabethan England, 1558–88: Preparing for your exam   103

Answers   109

Index   110

How to use this book

What's covered?

This book covers the British Depth study on Early Elizabethan England, 1558-88. This unit makes up 20% of your GCSE course, and will be examined in Paper 2.

Depth studies cover a short period of time, and require you to know about society, people and events in detail. You need to understand how the different aspects of the period fit together and affect each other. This book also explains the different types of exam questions you will need to answer, and includes advice and example answers to help you improve.

Features

As well as a clear, detailed explanation of the key knowledge you will need, you will also find a number of features in the book:

Key terms

Where you see a word followed by an asterisk, like this: Ecclesiastical*, you will be able to find a Key Terms box on that page that explains what the word means.

> **Key term**
>
> **Ecclesiastical***
> An adjective used to describe things to do with the Church.

Activities

Every few pages, you'll find a box containing some activities designed to help check and embed knowledge and get you to really think about what you've studied. The activities start simple, but might get more challenging as you work through them.

Summaries and Checkpoints

At the end of each chunk of learning, the main points are summarised in a series of bullet points – great for embedding the core knowledge, and handy for revision.

Checkpoints help you to check and reflect on your learning. The Strengthen section helps you to consolidate knowledge and understanding, and check that you've grasped the basic ideas and skills. The Challenge questions push you to go beyond just understanding the information, and into evaluation and analysis of what you've studied.

Sources and Interpretations

Although source work and interpretations do not appear in Paper 2, you'll still find interesting contemporary material throughout the books, showing what people from the period said, thought or created, helping you to build your understanding of people in the past.

The book also includes extracts from the work of historians, showing how experts have interpreted the events you've been studying.

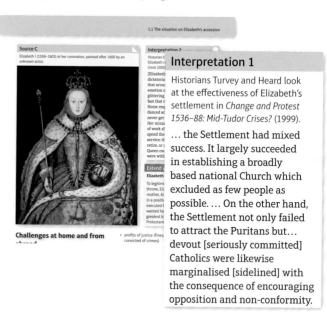

1.1 The situation on Elizabeth's accession

Source C
Elizabeth I (1558–1603) at her coronation, painted after 1600 by an unknown artist.

Challenges at home and from abroad

> **Interpretation 1**
>
> Historians Turvey and Heard look at the effectiveness of Elizabeth's settlement in *Change and Protest 1536–88: Mid-Tudor Crises?* (1999).
>
> … the Settlement had mixed success. It largely succeeded in establishing a broadly based national Church which excluded as few people as possible. … On the other hand, the Settlement not only failed to attract the Puritans but… devout [seriously committed] Catholics were likewise marginalised [sidelined] with the consequence of encouraging opposition and non-conformity.

Extend your knowledge

These features contain useful additional information that adds depth to your knowledge, and to your answers. The information is closely related to the key issues in the unit, and questions are sometimes included, helping you to link the new details to the main content.

> **Extend your knowledge**
>
> **North-West Passage**
>
> The discovery of the Americas had led to the belief that there was an alternative, faster and safer route via North America to the Pacific and the Far East. The search for this North-West Passage was another driving force behind the voyages of exploration and discovery during Elizabethan times. Although this passage was not discovered until 1845, explorers found out much more about the coastline of North America looking for it.

Exam-style questions and tips

The book also includes extra exam-style questions you can use to practise. These appear in the chapters and are accompanied by a tip to help you get started on an answer.

Exam-style question, Section B

Explain why the Catholic threat to Elizabeth I increased after 1566.

You may use the following in your answer:

- The Dutch Revolt
- Mary, Queen of Scots' arrival in England in 1568.

You must also use information of your own. **12 marks**

Exam tip

Don't just describe events. You must focus on reasons for the Catholic threat against Elizabeth becoming more serious.

Recap pages

At the end of each chapter, you'll find a page designed to help you to consolidate and reflect on the chapter as a whole. Each recap page includes a recall quiz, ideal for quickly checking your knowledge or for revision. Recap pages also include activities designed to help you summarise and analyse what you've learned, and also reflect on how each chapter links to other parts of the unit.

These activities are designed to help you develop a better understanding of how history is constructed, and are focused on the key areas of Evidence, Interpretations, Cause & Consequence and Change & Continuity. In the British Depth Study, you will come across activities on Cause & Consequence, as this is a key focus for this unit.

The Thinking Historically approach has been developed in conjunction with Dr Arthur Chapman and the Institute of Education, UCL. It is based on research into the misconceptions that can hold students back in history.

 Cause and Consequence (3c&d) — conceptual map reference

The Thinking Historically conceptual map can be found at: www.pearsonschools.co.uk/thinkinghistoricallygcse

WRITING HISTORICALLY

At the end of most chapters is a spread dedicated to helping you improve your writing skills. These include simple techniques you can use in your writing to make your answers clearer, more precise and better focused on the question you're answering.

The Writing Historically approach is based on the *Grammar for Writing* pedagogy developed by a team at the University of Exeter and popular in many English departments. Each spread uses examples from the preceding chapter, so it's relevant to what you've just been studying.

Preparing for your exams

At the back of the book, you'll find a special section dedicated to explaining and exemplifying the new Edexcel GCSE History exams. Advice on the demands of this paper, written by Angela Leonard, helps you prepare for and approach the exam with confidence. Each question type is explained through annotated sample answers at two levels, showing clearly how answers can be improved.

Pearson Progression Scale: This icon indicates the Step that a sample answer has been graded at on the Pearson Progression Scale.

This book is also available as an online ActiveBook, which can be licensed for your whole institution.

There is also an ActiveLearn Digital Service available to support delivery of this book, featuring a front-of-class version of the book, lesson plans, worksheets, exam practice PowerPoints, assessments, notes on Thinking Historically and Writing Historically, and more.

ActiveLearn
Digital Service

Timeline: Elizabethan England

Events at home

1558
Elizabeth I is crowned Queen of England after the death of her sister, Mary I

1559
Elizabeth implements her religious settlement, including the Act of Supremacy, Act of Uniformity and the Royal Injunctions

1563
Statute of Artificers

1568
Mary, Queen of Scots, flees to England from Scotland

1569
The Revolt of the Northern Earls to place Mary, Queen of Scots, on the throne

1570
Pope Pius V excommunicates Elizabeth from the Catholic Church

1571
The Ridolfi plot

1572
Vagabonds Act

1576
Poor Relief Act

1555   1560   1565   1570   1575

1559
Treaty of Cateau-Cambrésis

1560
Treaty of Edinburgh

1566
Dutch Revolt

1568
Genoese Loan

1576
The Spanish Fury

1576
Pacification of Ghent

1577–80
Francis Drake circumnavigates the world

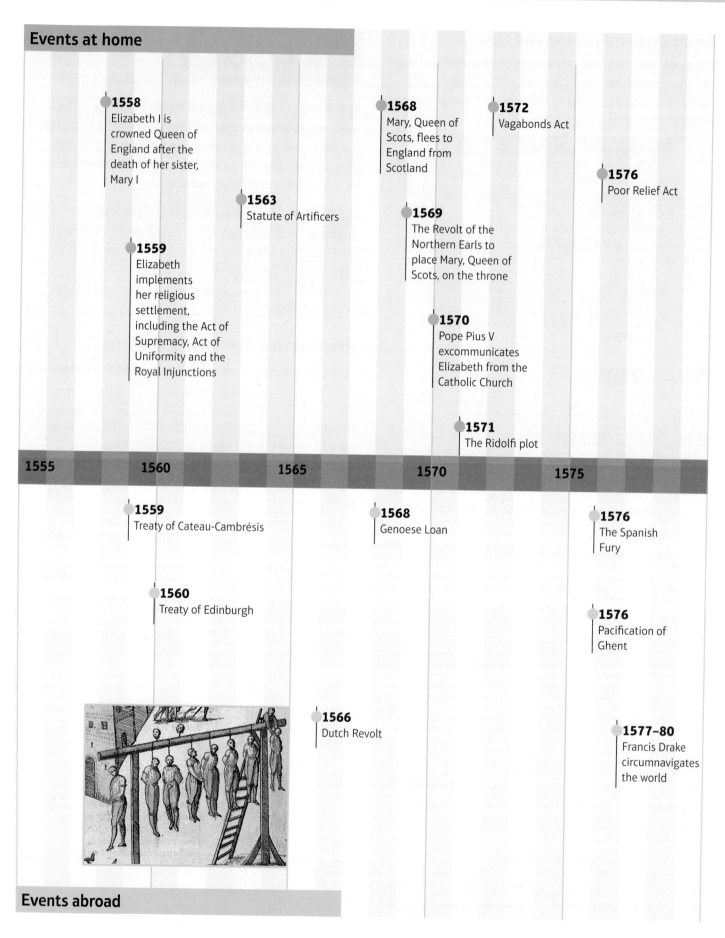

Events abroad

6

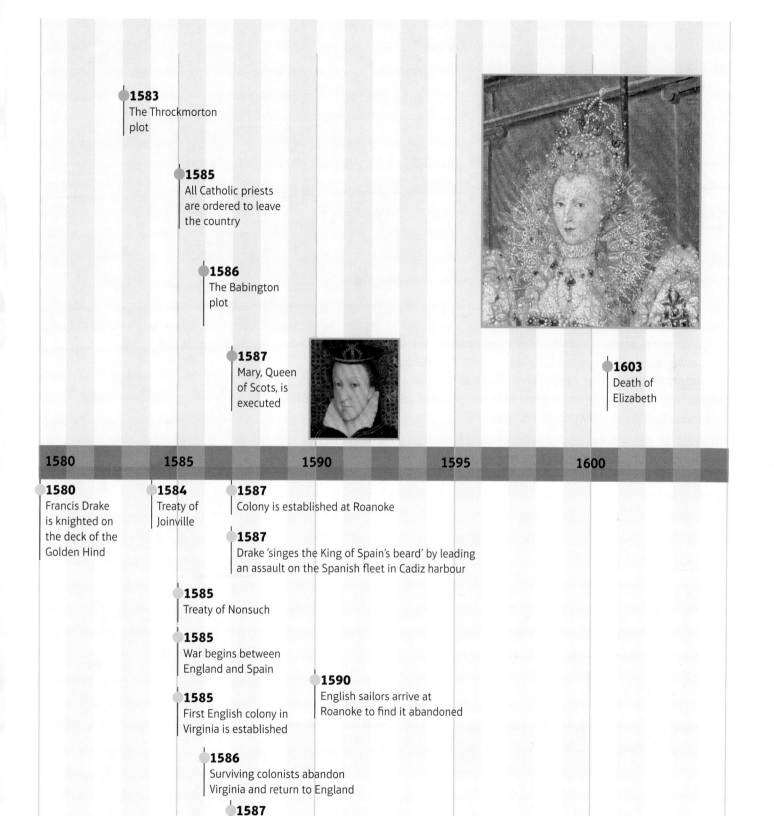

1583
The Throckmorton plot

1585
All Catholic priests are ordered to leave the country

1586
The Babington plot

1587
Mary, Queen of Scots, is executed

1603
Death of Elizabeth

| 1580 | 1585 | 1590 | 1595 | 1600 |

1580
Francis Drake is knighted on the deck of the Golden Hind

1584
Treaty of Joinville

1587
Colony is established at Roanoke

1587
Drake 'singes the King of Spain's beard' by leading an assault on the Spanish fleet in Cadiz harbour

1585
Treaty of Nonsuch

1585
War begins between England and Spain

1590
English sailors arrive at Roanoke to find it abandoned

1585
First English colony in Virginia is established

1586
Surviving colonists abandon Virginia and return to England

1587
Second attempt to colonise Roanoke

1588
Philip II of Spain launches the Armada
The Spanish are ultimately defeated at The Battle of Gravelines

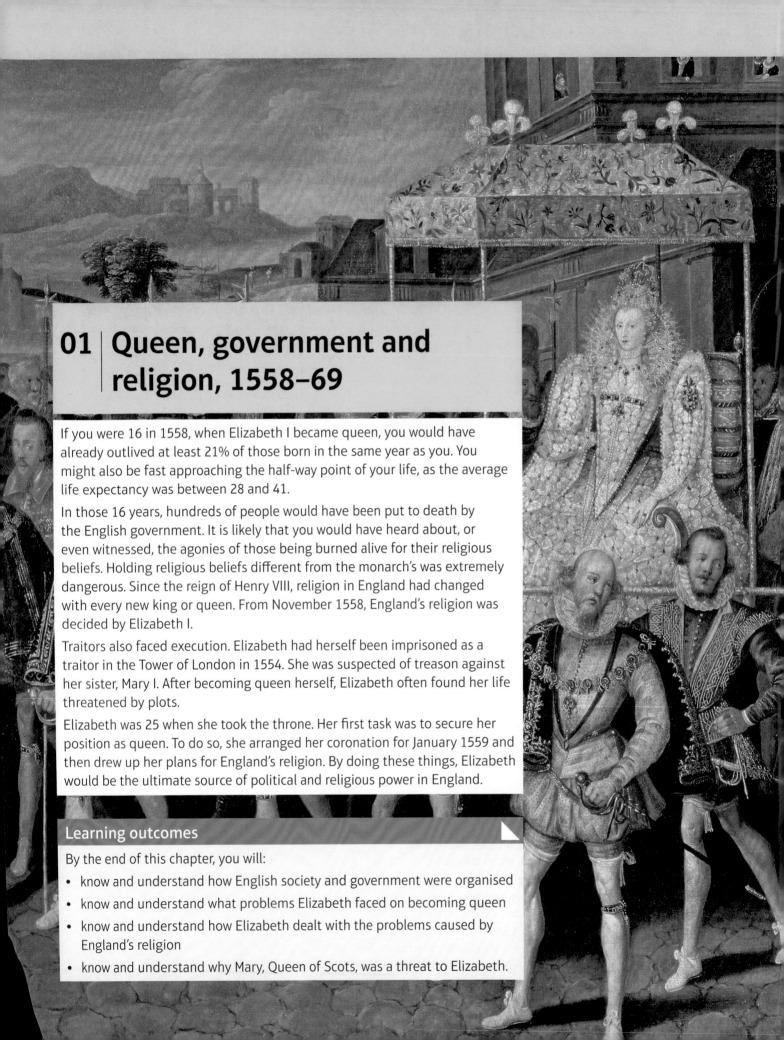

01 | Queen, government and religion, 1558–69

If you were 16 in 1558, when Elizabeth I became queen, you would have already outlived at least 21% of those born in the same year as you. You might also be fast approaching the half-way point of your life, as the average life expectancy was between 28 and 41.

In those 16 years, hundreds of people would have been put to death by the English government. It is likely that you would have heard about, or even witnessed, the agonies of those being burned alive for their religious beliefs. Holding religious beliefs different from the monarch's was extremely dangerous. Since the reign of Henry VIII, religion in England had changed with every new king or queen. From November 1558, England's religion was decided by Elizabeth I.

Traitors also faced execution. Elizabeth had herself been imprisoned as a traitor in the Tower of London in 1554. She was suspected of treason against her sister, Mary I. After becoming queen herself, Elizabeth often found her life threatened by plots.

Elizabeth was 25 when she took the throne. Her first task was to secure her position as queen. To do so, she arranged her coronation for January 1559 and then drew up her plans for England's religion. By doing these things, Elizabeth would be the ultimate source of political and religious power in England.

Learning outcomes

By the end of this chapter, you will:

- know and understand how English society and government were organised
- know and understand what problems Elizabeth faced on becoming queen
- know and understand how Elizabeth dealt with the problems caused by England's religion
- know and understand why Mary, Queen of Scots, was a threat to Elizabeth.

1.1 The situation on Elizabeth's accession

Learning outcomes

- Understand the structure of Elizabethan society in 1558.
- Understand the circumstances Elizabeth I found herself in when she came to the throne, including the issue of her legitimacy.
- Understand the challenges Elizabeth faced, both at home and abroad, during the early years of her reign.

Society and government in 1558

Elizabethan England was often a violent and dangerous place. As there was no police force or permanent army, keeping order relied upon a clear social structure in which everyone knew their place and had a role. Equality was not something that was important to Elizabethans. In fact, society, government, and law and order were based on inequality.

Society

Elizabethans had a very clear idea of where everyone belonged in society. The monarch was at the top of the social scale as the most important member of the **nobility**, followed by the rest of the nobility and **gentry**. Your place in this hierarchy was generally determined by how much land you had and whether you owned or rented it. About 90% of England's population lived and worked in the countryside. **Yeomen** were men who held a small amount of land or an estate – they were essentially lower gentry. **Tenant farmers** farmed rented land, which was usually owned by yeomen or the gentry.

In towns, the hierarchy was based on wealth and occupation. Wealthy **merchants** were at the top, followed by **professionals**, such as lawyers and doctors. Next came skilled craftsmen, such as silversmiths, glovers, carpenters or tailors, who could be quite wealthy business owners. They organised themselves into guilds, which were trade associations to monitor standards, working conditions and who were allowed to practise the trade. **Craftsmen** were skilled employees, and also included apprentices. **Unskilled labourers** and the unemployed came at the bottom of society.

Wherever you were in Elizabethan society, you owed respect and obedience to those above you and had a duty of care to those below you. Landowners ran their estates according to these ideas. Ideally they would take care of their tenants, especially during times of hardship.

Households were run along similar lines to society. The husband and father was head of the household. His wife, children and any servants were expected to be obedient to him.

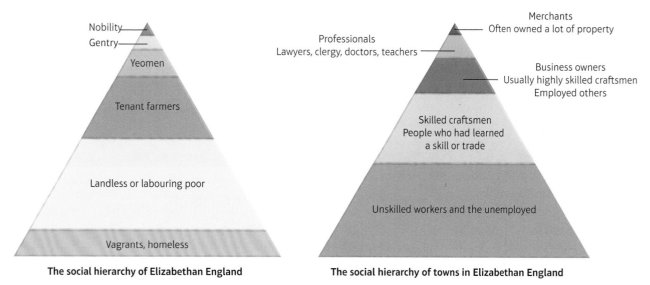

The social hierarchy of Elizabethan England

The social hierarchy of towns in Elizabethan England

Figure 1.1 Elizabethan society was a hierarchy in which everyone had a clear place in the social order.

Government

Elizabethan government had many key features. Different organisations had varying roles to keep Elizabethan England running smoothly.

Elizabethan Government		
What	**Key features**	**Role**
Court	The court was a body of people who lived in, or near the same palace or house as the monarch. The court was mostly made up of members of the nobility. They were the monarch's key servants, advisers and friends. Attending court required the monarch's permission.	• To entertain and advise the monarch • A public display of wealth and power • Courtiers* had influence with the monarch rather than actual power.
Privy Council	The Privy Council was made up of leading courtiers and advisers, as well as nobles and very senior government officials, like Sir William Cecil. There were approximately 19 members on the Privy Council, chosen by the monarch. They met at least three times a week, and the meetings were often attended and presided over by the monarch.	• To debate current issues and advise the monarch on government policy • Made sure the monarch's final decisions were carried out • Oversaw law and order, local government and the security of England • Monitored Justices of the Peace • Monitored the proceedings of Parliament.
Parliament	Parliament was made up of the House of Lords (which included bishops) and the House of Commons. Parliament could only be called and dismissed by the monarch. Elections were held before each new parliament, but very few people could vote. Elizabeth I called parliament ten times during her reign.	• To grant extraordinary taxation* • Passed laws (Acts of Parliament) • Offered advice to the monarch.
Lords Lieutenant	Each county had a Lord Lieutenant chosen by the monarch. They were members of the nobility and were often also on the Privy Council. They were essential to maintaining the monarch's power and England's defences.	• In charge of raising and training the local militia* and overseeing county defences • Oversaw the enforcement of policies • Part of the local government.
Justices of the Peace (JPs)	JPs were large landowners who kept law and order in their local areas. They were unpaid and they reported to the Privy Council. Being a JP was a position of status, and so was a very popular job.	• To make sure all social and economic policies were carried out • Heard county court cases every three months for more serious crimes • Part of the local government.

Key terms

Courtiers*

Were usually members of the nobility. Courtiers spent much of their lives with Elizabeth I.

Extraordinary taxation*

Occasional, additional taxation to pay for unexpected expenses, especially war.

Militia*

A military force of ordinary people, rather than soldiers, usually raised in an emergency.

The monarch

The government in Elizabethan England centred on the monarch. During, and even before, the Elizabethan period, monarchs of England believed they had the right to rule 'by the grace of God'. This was later known as divine right*. Because of this, Elizabeth I made government policy, making all the important decisions with the advice of her Privy Council. She could also:

- declare war and make peace
- call and dismiss parliament, and agree to, or reject, any laws they voted for
- rule in some legal cases, for example, if the law was unclear or if people appealed a judgement
- grant titles, lands, money, and jobs.

To provide someone with an important job or position is known as **patronage**. This could involve a grant of land, a title or championing a cause. Patronage is a very effective way of getting support from people and controlling them. What the queen gave, she could also take away if displeased. Other wealthy people could give patronage too, but the queen was the ultimate patron.*

The Secretary of State

Elizabeth's most important Privy Councillor was her Secretary of State. He was the person in government that she was closest to, and advised the queen on matters important to the Crown*. The most significant person to hold the position was Sir William Cecil, who held the position until 1573. He was later raised to the nobility and became Lord Burghley.

Key terms

Divine right*

Belief that the monarch's right to rule came from God.

Patron*

Someone who gives encouragement or financial support to an individual or a cause. For example, Elizabeth I was a patron of many explorers during her reign. She funded their voyages and publicly praised their efforts.

Crown*

With a capital 'C', the Crown refers to the monarch and their government.

Source A

Sir William Cecil (Lord Burghley from 1571), painted after 1587 by an unknown artist.

The monarch and parliament

Although the monarch had a regular income, there were often times when more was needed. Raising extraordinary taxation could only be done with parliament's agreement and so it was not possible to govern effectively without parliament.

Although the queen could issue direct orders (known as proclamations), they could not be enforced in England's law courts. Acts of Parliament, however, could be enforced and so any really important policies would be presented to parliament for its approval. Although, in theory, it was possible to vote against what the monarch wanted, this rarely happened. There were some areas that only the monarch had the right to decide upon. This was known as the **royal prerogative**. Elizabeth I claimed

Key term

Succession*

The issue of who was going to succeed the throne after the existing monarch died.

Extend your knowledge

Elizabethan parliament

Elizabeth's House of Commons was very different from today. There were no political parties, no prime minister and only wealthy men could vote or become members of parliament (MPs). Candidates for election were chosen by Privy Councillors. There were elections, although most were unchallenged.

Although MPs claimed the right to free speech, this did not prevent MPs from being sent to the Tower of London when it was decided, usually by the queen, that they had gone too far (they were always released). This meant that Elizabeth had considerable control over parliament.

Activity ?

Write a job advertisement for one of the roles in Elizabeth's government listed in the table above (see page 10). You should:

a describe the key features of the role

b explain what responsibilities the role involved

c describe why the job was important to the queen.

Ask a classmate to check the advertisement you have written, and suggest improvements.

it was her right as monarch to stop parliament discussing any issues she didn't want them to discuss. The most important of these included foreign policy, marriage and the succession*.

Source B

A drawing of Elizabeth I sitting in parliament. It is an English engraving from the 16th century. The queen's importance is shown by the size of her throne.

12

The Virgin Queen

Legitimacy

To inherit the throne, it was essential that the monarch was legitimate, which meant being born whilst the reigning king and queen were married (in wedlock). It was not possible for any child to inherit unless they were born in wedlock. Elizabeth I's legitimacy was in doubt because of how her father had divorced his first wife, Catherine of Aragon, in order to marry Elizabeth's mother, Anne Boleyn.

Henry VIII wanted to divorce Catherine in 1533 to marry Anne Boleyn, in the hope of getting a male heir. Catherine had given birth many times, but only one child had lived past infancy: a female heir, Mary. Henry wanted a male heir because he believed a woman could not rule the country with the same authority as a man. Henry believed Catherine could not give him the son he desperately wanted.

The head of the Roman Catholic* Church, the pope, refused to grant the divorce, leading to one of the most important developments in English history: the English Reformation. Henry VIII created the Church of England, separate from the Catholic Church, with himself as its head. He was then able to 'grant himself' a divorce (often referred to as an annulment). Henry married Anne Boleyn on 25 January 1533; Elizabeth was born on 7 September.

> **Key term**
>
> **Roman Catholic***
>
> The form of Christianity followed throughout the whole of Western Europe until the 16th century. A feature of Roman Catholicism includes allegiance to the pope, the head of the Catholic Church.

Committed Catholics refused to acknowledge Henry's divorce because the pope had not agreed to it. Catherine of Aragon was alive when Elizabeth was born, and so not everyone accepted that Elizabeth was legitimate. Some Catholics were even executed for refusing to accept her legitimacy.

In 1536, when Anne Boleyn was executed for treason, Henry VIII himself declared Elizabeth illegitimate and excluded her from the succession. However, he later reversed this decision.

Gender and marriage

A queen who ruled in her own right was something very unusual and it seemed unnatural to 16th-century society for a woman to rule. The Christian religion taught that women should be under the authority of men. Furthermore, monarchs were still expected to lead their armies into battle.

Figure 1.2 The pros and cons of Elizabeth marrying.

Women were not considered to be physically, mentally or emotionally capable of governing, and even the home was supposed to be under the authority of the husband or father. It was unusual for women to be in a position of power.

Many people thought that Elizabeth should marry. However, she had no intention of doing so. Elizabeth turned down offers from some of the most eligible princes of Europe, including her own brother-in-law, Philip II of Spain. Other failed suitors included King Eric of Sweden and the French heir to the throne, the Duke of Alençon.

The majority of people thought that women were not capable of ruling (see Interpretation 1). This prejudice had not been helped by Mary I's reign (1553–58). As England's first queen regnant* her short reign had not gone well.

- England had allied with Spain in a war against France and had lost. Morale was low.
- England's finances were poor and so were many of its people. There had been several bad harvests leading to disease, hunger and poverty.
- Mary's marriage to King Philip II of Spain was so unpopular that it had led to a rebellion.
- Mary burned almost 300 people for their religious beliefs. Although most people were Catholic, like Mary, the burnings had not been popular.

Key term

Queen regnant*

'Regnant' is a Latin word and means 'reigning'. Elizabeth was a queen regnant because she ruled in her own right, like her sister, Mary.

Character and strengths

Elizabeth was highly intelligent and well educated, with an eye for detail and an excellent grasp of politics. She spoke Latin, Greek, French and Italian. She had also experienced being a prisoner in the Tower of London, where she was held in 1554 on suspicion of treason against Mary I. She understood the dangerous world of court politics, where ambitious courtiers schemed and plotted to gain power and influence. The lifestyle for courtiers was lavish, but the stakes were high: fall out of favour with the queen and you could lose your life.

Elizabeth was confident and charismatic, able to make great speeches and win over her subjects, though she had a temper that people feared. She also often took a long time to make up her mind, especially over serious matters, and her Privy Council and advisers could find her extremely frustrating.

Activities ?

1 Working in pairs, write a quiz about Elizabeth I. The sections of the quiz should be 'The powers Elizabeth I had' and 'The problems Elizabeth I faced'. You must write out the questions and answers in full. Once you have finished, swap quizzes with another pair and answer the questions.

2 List the qualities that you think would make a successful 16th-century monarch.

3 Did Elizabeth I have these qualities? Make a table with two columns showing her strengths and weaknesses as a queen.

Interpretation 1

Historian Christopher Haigh interprets Elizabeth as a strong, independent female leader in the book *Elizabeth I* (1988).

Elizabeth sought to present herself, woman though she was, as a fit occupant of the throne of England, and she did not propose to confuse the issue by recruiting a husband or an heir. … This was done not by an attack upon the sixteenth century stereotype of a woman. Elizabeth accepted the image and often derided her own sex… she did not seek to change the ideal, but to escape from it, by suggesting that she was no ordinary woman.

Source C

Elizabeth I (1558–1603) at her coronation, painted after 1600 by an unknown artist.

Extend your knowledge

Elizabeth and Anne

To further legitimise her claim to the throne, Elizabeth campaigned for her mother, Anne Boleyn, to be remembered in a positive way. Anne Boleyn had been executed by Henry VIII, but Elizabeth wanted her to be remembered as his greatest love, and a martyr to her Protestant cause (see page 16).

Challenges at home and from abroad

Financial weakness

England's monarchs could not do whatever they pleased. They might rule by divine right, but they needed money and support to rule successfully. Monarchs could raise money from:

- rents and income from their own lands (Crown lands)
- taxes from trade (known as **customs duties**)
- special additional taxes known as subsidies, which had to be agreed by parliament

- profits of justice (fines, property or lands from people convicted of crimes)
- loans (sometimes loans were 'forced', meaning they were compulsory and never repaid).

Elizabeth's government did not have a lot of money, as England had fought costly wars before she became queen and lots of Crown lands had been sold off to raise money to fight them. When she took the throne, the Crown was £300,000 in debt, which was a huge sum in 1558. In contrast, the total annual income of the Crown at that time was approximately £286,667.

To be strong, Elizabeth had to be wealthy. Defending England and her throne was very expensive. Taxes were unpopular and parliament had to agree to them. In return, parliament could make demands on Elizabeth. She did not, therefore, want to have to rely too much on parliament for her income.

The French threat

France was wealthier and had a larger population than England. It was also England's traditional enemy and was an ally of England's other enemy, Scotland. Their friendship was known as the **Auld Alliance**. There was an added complication for Elizabeth: the Scottish monarch, Mary, Queen of Scots, was her cousin and had a strong claim to the English throne (see Figure 1.3 on page 17). She was also half French and married to Francis, heir to the French throne. She became queen of France in 1559 when her husband became King Francis II.

France and Scotland

Mary, Queen of Scots, declared herself the legitimate Catholic claimant to the English throne when Mary I died. Mary, Queen of Scots, was Elizabeth's second cousin, the granddaughter of Henry VIII's sister. Catholics who had not accepted Henry VIII's marriage to Anne Boleyn could rally to Mary, Queen of Scots' claim to be England's legitimate, Catholic monarch.

Scotland was an independent country and a traditional enemy of England. England's border with Scotland was remote and hard to defend, which meant it saw constant fighting and raids. In 1558, Mary's mother, Mary of Guise, was ruling Scotland for her daughter and had French troops stationed there.

France and Calais

England had held the French port of Calais since 1347. It was useful as it meant that England had a military base in France. It was also an important trading post. In the 1550s, England had sided with Spain in a war against the French, as Mary I was married to the Spanish king. In 1559, the conflict ended with the Treaty of Cateau-Cambrésis. Under this treaty, England had to return Calais to France. The English felt humiliated by this loss, and so regaining Calais was an important aim of Elizabeth's foreign policy when she became queen. By regaining Calais, Elizabeth could right the mistake of Mary I. She could also reclaim some of the glory enjoyed by past monarchs, who had successfully held Calais as an English outpost in France for hundreds of years.

Elizabeth was also concerned that France and Spain were no longer at war. Although the two powers were great rivals, they were both Roman Catholic countries. Countries took their monarch's religion and Elizabeth was Protestant. Protestants were Christians, but did not accept the pope as their religious leader. Nor did they agree with some Catholic teachings, such as clergy not being allowed to marry, or church services and the Bible only being in Latin. Divisions between Protestants and Catholics were already causing conflict in Europe. There was a real possibility that Catholic Spain and France would unite against England and its Protestant queen.

Activities

1   Add a section to the quiz which you began on page 14 to test others in your class on foreign threats to Elizabeth I.

2   Identify and explain the three most important problems faced by Elizabeth I on becoming queen.

3   Look back at your work on the powers Elizabeth had as queen and the strengths she had as a person. Work with two or three of your classmates to draw up an action plan for her to tackle the three problems you identified in Q2. Present it to the class.

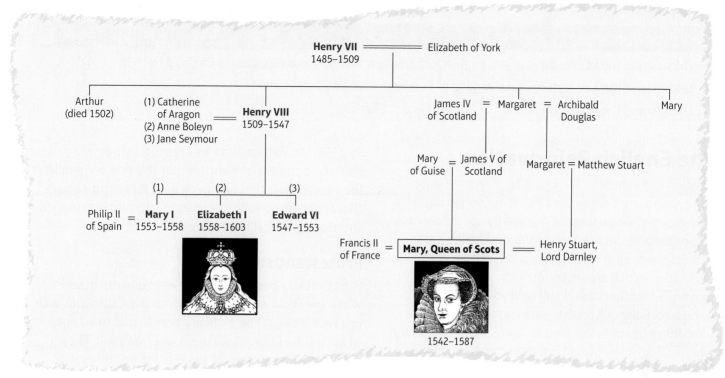

Figure 1.3 Elizabeth I's family tree showing Mary, Queen of Scots' claim to the English throne.

Summary

- Elizabeth I was only England's second ruling queen and it was thought unnatural for women to rule alone.
- Elizabeth was highly intelligent, educated and charismatic, but could be indecisive.
- Elizabeth was the head of the government and made all the key decisions.
- However, she also needed her Privy Council, parliament, Lord Lieutenants and JPs to govern effectively.
- The monarch decided what the country's religion would be.
- England faced possible threats from France, Scotland and Spain.
- Elizabeth's claim to the throne was doubted by some Catholics who looked to her cousin, the Catholic Mary, Queen of Scots, as a possible heir or potential alternative ruler.

Checkpoint

Strengthen

S1 Give two issues Elizabeth I faced over her suitability to rule England.

S2 Give at least two ways in which the Privy Council, parliament and JPs were important in governing England.

S3 Describe Elizabeth I's strengths and weaknesses as a monarch.

Challenge

C1 Explain how at least two factors combined to make governing England a problem for Elizabeth I. For example, gender and politics; foreign and domestic issues.

C2 Explain how a combination of factors made the defence of England a problem for Elizabeth I.

If you are not confident about any of these questions, form a group with other students, discuss the answers and then record your conclusions. Your teacher can give you some hints.

1.2 The 'settlement' of religion

The English Reformation

Religion was central to life in the 16th century. Until 1517, Catholicism dominated Western Europe. Baptism, marriage and death were all marked by special services and ceremonies. Confession of sins and taking part in mass* were vital to keeping your soul from eternal damnation in hell and, even after you were dead, prayers from others could still help you on your way to heaven. Religious festivals marked the agricultural year. These festivals included Plough Sunday in January, where ploughs were traditionally blessed, and the Harvest Festival, which gave thanks for a plentiful harvest. Religion guided people's morals and behaviour as well as their understanding of the world.

The Reformation* began in Europe because a growing number of people believed that the Roman Catholic Church had become corrupt, greedy and no longer represented a truly Christian life: it needed to be reformed. This led some people, known as Protestants, to abandon the Roman Catholic faith altogether and establish their own Churches, without the pope.

The English Reformation began in 1532, when Henry VIII created the Church of England. However, Henry was never a true Protestant – his changes came out of his desire to divorce his first wife.

By 1558, the Reformation was tearing Europe apart. It is hard to appreciate the impact that this had on people at the time. Beliefs that had been held for centuries were challenged and this threatened to overturn established social and political hierarchies.

Protestantism

Most ordinary people could not read or write in Latin. When the Bible was only in Latin, as the Catholic Church believed it should be, ordinary people had to accept whatever the Church told them was God's will. They had no power to interpret the Bible in any other way. Protestants believed that the Bible should be translated into their own languages so that people were able to more easily engage with their religion.

Once people were able to understand and study the Bible for themselves, some more extreme Protestants wanted to base their religion solely on what was in the Bible. Few of the traditional church ceremonies and decorations were in the Bible. Nor were certain Church offices, such as bishops, so why were they needed?

Under a threat this serious, the Roman Catholic Church focused on strengthening the Catholic faith. Many countries were divided, leading to persecution and even civil and religious wars.

Key terms

Mass*

Roman Catholic service at which Catholics are given bread and wine. Catholics believe that this involves a miracle: the bread and wine is turned into the body and blood of Christ.

The Reformation*

A challenge to the teachings and power of the Roman Catholic Church. This movement is said to have begun in Europe in 1517.

Source A

The title page of Elizabeth I's personal Bible, given to her in 1568. It was written in English.

The Reformation: comparing Roman Catholicism and Protestantism	
Roman Catholicism	**Protestantism**
• The pope is the head of the Church.	• There should not be a pope.
• Underneath the pope are cardinals, archbishops, bishops and priests.	• It is not necessary to have cardinals, or even archbishops or bishops.
• The Bible and church services should be in Latin.	• The Bible and church services should be in your own language.
• The Church acts as an intermediary* between God and the people.	• People have their own, direct relationship with God through prayer and Bible study.
• The Church can forgive sins.	• Sins can only be forgiven by God.
• During mass a miracle occurs when the bread and wine become the body and blood of Christ.	• The bread and wine simply represent the Last Supper* in the Bible. There is no miracle.
• Priests are special and should wear special clothing (vestments).	• Priests are not special and should not wear special clothing.
• Churches should be highly decorated in honour and glory of God.	• Churches should be plain and simple so as not to distract from worshipping God.
• There are seven sacraments.*	• There are only two sacraments: baptism and Holy Communion*.
• Priests are forbidden to marry.	• Priests are permitted to marry if they wished.

Religious divisions in England in 1558

Elizabeth I was a Protestant. However, historians now believe that when she became queen in 1558, most of her subjects were Catholic. Edward VI (1547–53), Elizabeth's brother, was the only true Protestant monarch England had ever had. Henry VIII was head of the Church of England but had never really accepted most Protestant beliefs, and Elizabeth's sister, Mary I, had faced very little opposition to making England Roman Catholic again.

There was a great deal of religious conflict spreading through Europe as Roman Catholics and Protestants fought to establish their faith as the 'true' religion. Elizabeth feared this conflict would spread to England, and for good reason. Catholics who had not accepted Henry VIII's divorce from Catherine of Aragon believed Elizabeth to be illegitimate and therefore that she had no right to be queen. There was also a Roman Catholic alternative for the English throne, Elizabeth's cousin Mary, Queen of Scots.

*The clergy**

In 1558, most of England's bishops were Catholic. Changing the religion of the country needed an Act of Parliament. The House of Commons would be likely to agree with what Elizabeth wanted, but there were lots of Catholic bishops in the House of Lords. Although many priests changed their religion to keep their jobs, others were committed Catholics and would not agree to work in a Protestant Church.

Key terms

Intermediary*

Someone who acts as a go-between when direct communication is not possible.

Last Supper*

The last meal that Christ shared with his disciples (followers). Commemorating it is very important to Christians as it is a reminder that Christ sacrificed his life to save humanity.

Sacraments*

Special Church ceremonies.

Holy Communion*

Another name for mass, often used in Protestant churches.

Clergy*

Religious leaders, such as bishops and priests.

Key terms

Diocese*

An area looked after by a bishop.

German states*

Germany did not exist in the 16th century. There were, however, many (usually small) states where German was spoken but they were independent of each other. These states formed part of the Holy Roman Empire (see page 28).

Activities   ?

1. Imagine you are Elizabeth I. Explain what it is you dislike about:
   a. The Roman Catholic religion
   b. The Puritan religion.

2. Identify the problems Elizabeth I would face in establishing her Protestant religion in England. Remember that she needs to get parliament to agree to it and then has to make sure that the people obey it.

3. Are there any ways around the problems Elizabeth I faced? What could she do to ensure England's religion could be changed without causing unrest or rebellion?

Geographical divisions

Parts of England were more Catholic than others, meaning the people living there were less likely to accept Protestantism. These areas, such as Lancashire, tended to be further from London. Parts of the north, west and diocese* such as Lichfield were especially Catholic. The more remote a community, the more likely it was to be Catholic.

London, East Anglia and the south-east tended to be more Protestant. They had closer links with the Netherlands and the German states* where Protestantism had become popular. Therefore, Protestant books and ideas often came into England through London and the south-east, where they spread.

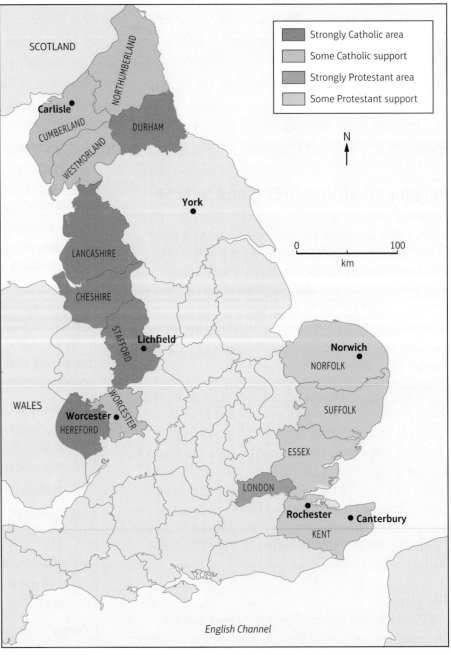

Figure 1.4 English and Welsh diocese at the time of Elizabeth I.

Puritans

When Mary I was queen of England, approximately 300 Protestants were burned for their religious beliefs. Many more escaped into exile in more tolerant Protestant states on the continent, such as the Netherlands. They returned to England when Elizabeth inherited the throne as much more committed Protestants with more radical (extreme) beliefs.

Radical Protestants were often referred to as **Puritans** because they wanted to 'purify' the Christian religion by getting rid of anything that wasn't in the Bible. Puritan congregations wanted to manage their own churches themselves, rather than bishops or the pope choosing for them. However, under that system, there was no role for the monarch as head of the Church, either. Furthermore, Puritan churches would be very basic, without even the altars* or special clothes for priests that could be found in some Protestant churches and that Elizabeth I liked.

Key term

Altars*

The table in a church where mass is performed.

Elizabeth's religious settlement, 1559

Elizabeth wanted to find a compromise when it came to England's religion. This meant establishing a form of Protestantism that Catholics could accept. Elizabeth ruled out a Puritan religion as she didn't want to turn her Catholic subjects against her. Personally, Elizabeth herself did not believe in the extreme Protestantism practised by Puritans. Puritans also wanted to develop their own Church, under their own leadership, which would challenge her authority as queen. It was generally believed in the 16th century that successful governments needed the country to follow the monarch's religion. If not, to whom would people turn to as the ultimate source of authority: the monarch or the Church? There were some Puritans who believed that, in some circumstances, subjects had the right to overthrow their monarchs.

Features of the religious settlement

Elizabeth I's religious settlement was designed to be accepted by as many of her subjects as possible, be they Catholic or Protestant. The religious settlement was established in 1559 and came in three parts.

- The **Act of Supremacy** made Elizabeth supreme governor of the Church of England – all clergy and royal officials had to swear an oath of allegiance to her as the head of the Church.
- The **Act of Uniformity** established the appearance of churches and the form of services they held.
- The **Royal Injunctions** was a set of instructions, issued by Sir William Cecil on behalf of the queen to the clergy, on a wide range of issues to reinforce the acts of Supremacy and Uniformity. It included instructions on how people should worship God and the structure of services.

Under the Act of Supremacy, an Ecclesiastical* High Commission was established with the job of maintaining discipline within the church and enforcing the queen's religious settlement. Members of the clergy whose loyalty was in doubt could be punished.

The Act of Uniformity introduced a set form of church service in the Book of Common Prayer to be used in **all** churches. The clergy had to use the wording of the Prayer Book when conducting services. Anyone who refused to use it was punished. The wording of the service was deliberately unclear so that, for example, Catholics could take it as meaning the bread and wine became the body and blood of Christ, while Protestants could take it as simply an act of remembrance. It also made it clear that priests were to wear special clothing.

Key term

Ecclesiastical*

An adjective used to describe things to do with the Church.

Extend your knowledge

Transubstantiation

Term meaning that the bread and wine that form the central part of a Catholic Church service become the body and blood of Christ. They are **trans**formed. This does not mean that they change appearance and texture, but that Christ is present in them. Protestants didn't believe in it.

Key terms

Royal Supremacy*

This is when the monarch is head of the Church.

Pilgrimage*

A journey to an important religious monument, shrine or place.

Saints*

A saint is someone who lived an exceptional, holy life. To be made a saint by the Catholic Church, several conditions have to be met, including having lived a good life.

Interpretation 1

Historians Turvey and Heard look at the effectiveness of Elizabeth's settlement in *Change and Protest 1536–88: Mid-Tudor Crises?* (1999).

… the Settlement had mixed success. It largely succeeded in establishing a broadly based national Church which excluded as few people as possible. … On the other hand, the Settlement not only failed to attract the Puritans but… devout [seriously committed] Catholics were likewise marginalised [sidelined] with the consequence of encouraging opposition and non-conformity.

The Act of Uniformity also ordered that everyone was to attend church on a Sunday and other holy days, such as Good Friday, or else be fined one shilling for every absence. There were 12 pence in a shilling. Although earnings varied widely, the Labourers' Act of 1563 said that:

- labourers could earn up to three pence a day
- skilled craftsmen could earn up to four pence a day
- a servant could earn between eight and nine pence a week.

Therefore, for many people, a fine for not attending church on a Sunday could total a week's pay. For the nobility, however, a shilling would not be a serious amount of money.

The Royal Injunctions were issued to help further establish the Acts of Supremacy and Uniformity. They covered a range of issues, including:

- all clergy were to teach the Royal Supremacy*
- anyone who refused to attend church was to be reported to the Privy Council
- each parish was to have a copy of the Bible in English
- no one was allowed to preach without a licence from the government
- pilgrimages* and monuments to 'fake' miracles were banned
- the clergy were to wear special vestments.

Pilgrimages to places where saints* were buried, or where miracles were supposed to have happened, were important to the Catholic religion. To Protestants, this was all superstition. The Royal Injunctions referred to 'fake' miracles, leaving the possibility that there might be real ones (although none had yet been found). This could have helped to make Elizabeth I's religious settlement more widely acceptable. The Royal Injunctions also allowed images in churches. This would help keep their familiar look for worshippers, again helping to make Elizabeth I's changes less unsettling. Puritans, however, especially disliked people praying before saints' statues, as the Bible forbade worshipping idols. Traditionally, idols were images or representations of gods. Puritans believed people should only pray to the one true God, and that praying to idols was a sin.

Exam-style question, Section B

Describe **two** features of the Elizabethan religious settlement. **4 marks**

Exam tip

The answer must give some supporting information for both examples. You will get a mark for each feature, and a mark for supporting each feature with one additional piece of information. Make your points clearly in fully developed sentences and then move on to the next question.

Key
1. Altar, which is set apart from the congregation
2. Ornate robes
3. Painted walls depicting Bible stories
4. Stained glass window
5. Elaborate crucifix and statues of saints

Figure 1.5 Traditional Catholic church in the reign of Mary I.

Key
1. Plain table instead of an altar
2. Simple robes
3. No ornate decoration
4. Plain windows
5. Royal crest instead of religious decoration

Figure 1.6 Protestant church in Elizabethan England.

The impact of the religious settlement

Elizabeth wanted a Protestant Church that Catholics could accept. She did not want them to feel forced to choose between loyalty to their religion and their queen, so she wanted to keep a Catholic 'feel' to churches. As long as people conformed outwardly, Elizabeth did not want persecution. She hoped that the Catholic faith would simply fade away in England as the old clergy died out. Interpretation 1 (see page 22) sees the Elizabethan religious settlement as successful – up to a point.

The clergy

All members of the Church had to take the oath of supremacy under the Act of Supremacy if they were to keep their posts. Eight thousand priests and less important clergy did so. There were approximately 10,000 parishes in England at this time, so this shows that the religious settlement was largely successful.

When it came to the bishops, however, only one agreed to take the oath. The others all had to step down and Elizabeth appointed 27 new bishops. This gave her the opportunity to put Protestants in place. She could not afford to lose the support of these new bishops, as there was a shortage of qualified Protestant clergy in England.

The people

The majority of ordinary people accepted Elizabeth's religious settlement and attended the Church of England services, even though many of them held on to Catholic beliefs. The wording of the new Prayer Book helped this because it could be understood to mean different things by Catholics and Protestants according to their beliefs.

Parishes in places like Lancashire, where Catholics were in the majority, were slow to change to the new services, however. Nevertheless, Elizabeth made it clear that she did not want the settlement enforced too strongly, even if people were recusants*.

In most of the country, the change of religion was smooth. However, in some places, Protestants welcomed the new Elizabethan religious settlement with sometimes violent enthusiasm. In London, for example, there was a great deal of destruction of church ornaments and statues of saints.

Key term

Recusants*

Catholics who were unwilling to attend church services laid down by the Elizabethan religious settlement.

Extend your knowledge

Continuing Catholicism

There were ways around the Elizabethan religious settlement for committed Catholics. For example, many attended church but then had private Catholic services in their homes. Sometimes the husband and father would go to Church of England services, but his wife and children would stay at home to say their prayers and practise Catholic beliefs. This meant they avoided fines.

Source B

Written by an observer attending an open-air preaching event at Dedham, Essex, in 1575. He describes the impact of the preacher.

... at Dedham men hang weeping on the necks of their horses after Mr. Rogers's sermon had acted out a little scene in which God threatened to take away the Bible from the English people.

The role of the Church of England

The parish church was a central point of village life, and religion could have a massive impact upon people, stirring up great emotion (as shown in Source B).

Church courts

Although Church courts mainly focused on Church matters, they did act in a range of minor disputes on moral issues. Examples of moral issues dealt with by the Church included marriage (ensuring both bride and groom were marrying of their own free will, or at a suitable age), sexual offences (such as bigamy – being married to more than one person at the same time), and slander (false insults). Church courts also dealt with wills and inheritance. For example, all wills had to be proved valid before anyone could inherit. Lawyers greatly resented the powers that the Church courts had.

All other offences, such as civil cases (one person suing another), disputes over land, robbery, fraud, rape and murder were dealt with in the ordinary court system.

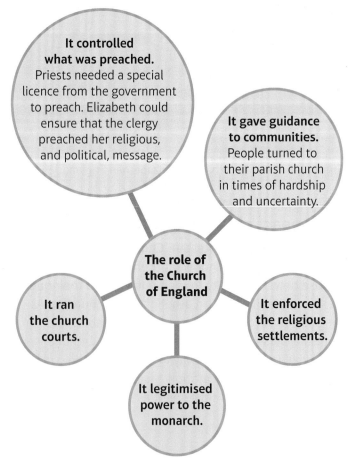

Figure 1.7 The role of the Church of England.

24

Enforcing the settlement

The Church was responsible for helping to enforce the religious settlement. Visitations were inspections of churches and clergy by bishops to ensure that everyone took the oath of supremacy and were following the terms of the religious settlement.

The first visitations were in 1559 and resulted in up to 400 clergy being dismissed. In some places, those carrying out the visitations caused a great deal of destruction of decorations and statues in churches, which was more action than Elizabeth wanted. In addition, she made it clear that she did not want people's religious beliefs investigated too closely.

After 1559, visitations took place every three to four years. They were very wide-ranging and did not just cover the Church. For example, not only did clergy have to present their preaching licences, but teachers, midwives, surgeons and physicians had to provide the licences that allowed them to practise their jobs. In this way, the Church was able to monitor other professions for the government.

Activities ?

1 Draw up a table with three columns: 'Catholic', 'Protestant' and 'Enforcement'. In each column, list as many features of the religious settlement as you can that (i) pleased Catholics; (ii) pleased Protestants; (iii) helped the government enforce the settlement.

2 Design a leaflet that informs the English people on what they need to know about the religious settlement. There should be sections on: what the queen's aims are; what churches and church services will be like; what all loyal subjects are supposed to do; and how the religious settlement will be enforced.

Summary

- Elizabeth was a Protestant queen but England was not a completely Protestant country.
- More Protestant areas of the country were London, the south-east and East Anglia, while Catholicism was especially strong in the north and west of England.
- The religious settlement came in three parts: the Act of Supremacy, the Act of Uniformity and the Royal Injunctions.
- In some places, changing over to the new religious settlement was very slow.
- Visitations enforced the religious settlement but Elizabeth ordered them not to be too harsh.

Checkpoint

Strengthen

S1 What were Elizabeth's main aims in her religious settlement?

S2 What two Acts of Parliament were part of the religious settlement and what did they say?

S3 What were the Royal Injunctions?

S4 What was the role of the Church of England in enforcing the religious settlement?

Challenge

C1 Which key features of the religious settlement appealed to:
  - Catholics
  - Protestants?

C2 What evidence is there that Elizabeth's religious settlement:
  - was very popular
  - was not very popular?

If you are not confident about any of these questions, discuss the possible answers in pairs and then record your conclusions. Your teacher can give you some hints.

1.3 Challenge to the religious settlement

Learning outcomes

- Understand the nature and extent of the Puritan challenge to Elizabeth I.
- Understand the nature and extent of the threat of the Catholic Church, including the Revolt of the Northern Earls.
- Understand the nature and extent of the threat of foreign powers to Elizabeth I.

The nature and extent of the Puritan challenge

Puritans hoped that Elizabeth I's religious reforms would be the beginning of further, more Protestant developments to the Church of England. For Elizabeth, however, the issue of religion in England had been dealt with. During the 1560s, the main Puritan challenge to the religious settlement came from within the Church of England itself, and especially the bishops.

It was not long before Puritan clergymen began ignoring or disobeying parts of the religious settlement. Elizabeth's aim of uniformity in the conduct of Church services was not met: for example, should people kneel to receive communion? Some clergy wanted the abolition of organ music accompanying hymns and certain holy days (which would not please ordinary people, especially when the holy day was a holiday). This all represented a direct challenge to her authority as Supreme Governor of the Church of England. The two biggest issues were over **crucifixes** and **clothing**.

The crucifix controversy

A crucifix is an image of Jesus Christ dying on the cross. The cross is the symbol of the Christian religion because Jesus was executed by crucifixion in about 33 CE.

To Elizabethan Puritans, crucifixes represented idols. Elizabeth, however, liked them and also wanted churches to keep their familiar look and feel. This was an important part of her religious settlement because she didn't want to anger her Catholic subjects by changing too much too fast. She therefore demanded that each church should display a crucifix. When some Puritan bishops threatened to resign, the queen backed down.

She was unable to enforce her will in this instance, as she could not afford to ignore their concerns. There weren't yet enough able Protestant clergymen to take the place of any bishops who were dismissed. Nevertheless, she insisted on keeping a crucifix in the Royal Chapel.

The vestment controversy

What priests wore was another issue for Puritans. Some thought that they should not have special clothing at all. Others believed that it should be very plain and simple. Elaborate vestments suggested that priests were set apart from ordinary people. In the Catholic faith they *were* special. Priests had the power to turn the bread and wine into the body and blood of Christ. They could also forgive sins. However, this is not what Protestants believed.

Source A

Puritan father teaching his family. This woodcut picture was made in 1563.

Elizabeth wanted the clergy to wear special vestments as set out in the Royal Injunctions. By 1565, it was clear that not all clergy were wearing what the queen had commanded. Some were also not following instructions on how to conduct services properly. In 1566, the archbishop of Canterbury, Matthew Parker, issued further guidelines for priests in his 'Book of Advertisements'. These followed Elizabeth's commands. He also held a special exhibition in London to show priests what vestments they must wear and when. Of the 110 invited, 37 refused to attend and lost their posts. Unlike the crucifix controversy, the majority of priests consented to Elizabeth's insistence that special vestments must be worn, despite some opposition.

The nature and extent of the Catholic challenge

The papacy*

Although the Catholic Church was trying to tackle the spread of Protestantism by dealing with corruption and other problems throughout Europe, it was also leading an active fight back to strengthen Catholicism by supporting local communities, persecuting heretics* and encouraging the waging of war against Protestants. This campaign against Protestantism was known as the **Counter-Reformation**.

Although the papacy did not offer much leadership to English Catholics, in 1566 the pope issued an instruction that they should not attend Church of England services.

Although there were penalties for those who did not conform to the religious settlement, they were generally not imposed. However, punishments for repeat offenders included fines, imprisonment, or loss of property, job and even life, depending upon the crime. However, the authorities were ordered not to investigate recusants too closely: Elizabeth did not want to create martyrs* and preferred to ignore smaller examples of disobedience. As a result, England was stable in the first decade of her reign (see Interpretation 1).

Key terms

Papacy*
The system of Church government ruled by the pope.

Heretics*
People who have controversial opinions and beliefs at odds with those held by the rest of society, but especially those who deny the teachings of the Catholic Church.

Martyr*
Someone who is killed for his or her beliefs, especially religious beliefs.

Interpretation 1

From *The Reign of Elizabeth: England 1558–1603*, Barbara Mervyn talks about the effectiveness of Elizabeth's religious policies (2001).

By 1568, Elizabeth's policies seemed to be working. The early problems caused by the settlement seemed to be fading. The majority of Catholics outwardly conformed and, without any leadership from the Pope, were politically loyal.

England's nobility and the Catholic threat

It is difficult to know how acceptable English Catholics really found the Elizabethan Church. It is estimated, however, that one-third of the nobility and a sizeable number of the gentry were recusants, especially in the north-west of England. The nobility who remained Catholic tended to be from ancient families, especially in the north of England. The earls of Northumberland and Westmorland, for example, had been prosperous under Mary I. When Elizabeth I became queen, they found their influence at court greatly reduced. They disliked her favourites, such as Robert Dudley, Earl of Leicester, and Sir William Cecil. Elizabeth's favourites tended to be Protestant and either from new noble families (Dudley) or not noble at all (Cecil).

In November 1569, the earls of Northumberland and Westmorland led a rebellion in the north of England against Elizabeth known as the Revolt of the Northern Earls (see Chapter 2). One of the key events of the rebellion was the taking of Durham Cathedral and the celebration of a full Catholic mass.

Even though the earls' reasons for rebelling stemmed from a lack of political power and influence under Elizabeth I, the Catholic religion brought many other northerners to their cause. Rallied by this support, the rebels marched south. By 22 November, they controlled the land east of the Pennines as far south as Braham Moor, north of Leeds.

The earls of Northumberland and Westmorland appealed to the Catholic nobility, especially in Lancashire and Cheshire, but they did not join them. The vast majority of England's nobles stayed loyal to Elizabeth, with the exception of the Duke of Norfolk, England's most senior noble and her distant cousin. On 24 November 1569, the rebels were forced to retreat.

The rebellion was successfully put down by royal troops under the leadership of the Earl of Sussex. Nevertheless, Elizabeth's reaction to it shows how dangerous she believed it was. Hundreds of rebels were executed in towns and cities across the north. These public displays of Crown power mark a change in Elizabeth's relationship with her Catholic subjects, which was to become even more difficult in the 1570s.

Foreign powers

England was not the only place in Europe where Protestantism was taking root. Scotland, France, parts of the Holy Roman Empire* and the Netherlands (which belonged to Spain) all had growing Protestant populations.

However, Europe was dominated by Catholic powers determined to limit the spread of Protestantism. One of the greatest of these was the Habsburg family, who controlled both the Spanish and Austrian empires, and also the Holy Roman Empire, during Elizabeth's reign. Although each of these was ruled by competing family members, defending the Catholic faith was one cause that could unite them.

France

When religious war broke out in France in 1562, Elizabeth I was concerned about its potential to threaten her realm by encouraging religious conflict in England. She wrote to Philip II of Spain on the matter in 1564, explaining how 'troubled and perplexed' she was.

Elizabeth had agreed in 1562 to help French Protestants, hoping to get back Calais in return. She had already successfully helped Scottish Protestant lords rebel against Catholic rule in 1560 (see page 32). This time, however, her policy failed. The French Protestants made peace with the Catholics later in 1562.

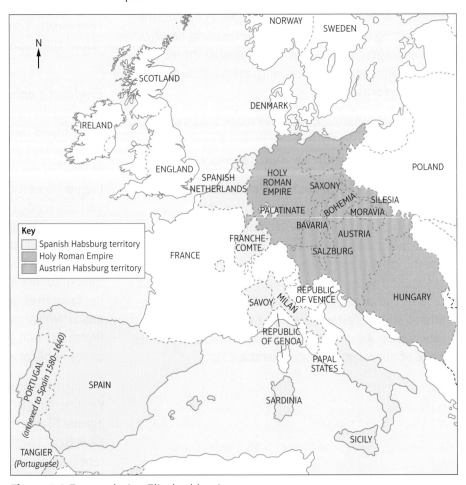

Figure 1.8 Europe during Elizabeth's reign.

In 1564, Elizabeth signed the Treaty of Troyes, confirming once and for all that Calais belonged to France. All that she had ultimately achieved was to irritate Philip II of Spain by supporting Protestant rebels.

Spain and the Spanish Netherlands

In the 16th century, the Netherlands belonged to the Spanish king, Philip II. He was a strict Roman Catholic and did not look favourably upon Elizabeth's support for Protestant rebels in Scotland and France. In fact, in 1563, he banned the import of English cloth to the Netherlands as he believed that English merchants were encouraging the spread of Protestantism there. Elizabeth retaliated and ceased trading with the Netherlands. This trade embargo* affected both countries economically and only lasted a year. For her part, Elizabeth was concerned that Spain and France might form an alliance against her. In the 1530s, Pope Paul III had excommunicated* Henry VIII after the break from Rome* and had then asked France and Spain to invade England and depose him.

Extend your knowledge

Philip II of Spain

Although his wife, Mary I, had just died, Philip II proposed a marriage alliance with Elizabeth I when she came to the throne. This suggests that he still valued England as an ally. Elizabeth refused him.

Key terms

Trade embargo*

When governments ban trade with another country.

Excommunicated*

A very severe punishment, imposed by the pope, expelling people from the Catholic Church.

Rome*

Capital of Italy – but also used to mean the pope or the Catholic Church.

Spanish Inquisition*

A political and religious body set up by Spain in 1478 to keep Spanish territories true to the Catholic faith. Anyone caught by the Inquisition who wasn't Catholic could be tortured or burned alive in a public execution.

The Dutch Revolt

Since the 1550s, there had been growing unhappiness in the Netherlands about Spanish interference in Dutch affairs. Although the Netherlands belonged to Spain, they were used to governing themselves. When Philip II decided to reorganise the Dutch government and Church, he also brought the Spanish Inquisition* to the Netherlands. These actions united both Catholics and Protestants against Spain, leading to the Dutch Revolt, which broke out for the first time in 1566. In 1567, Philip sent the Duke of Alba with an army of 10,000 men to the Netherlands to put down the revolt. By 1568, it had been defeated.

Alba established a Council of Troubles in the Netherlands (nicknamed the Council of Blood) to enforce both Catholicism and obedience to the Spanish Crown. It was made up of loyal Dutch nobles and Spanish officials. It ignored local law and legal processes, condemning thousands to death (mainly Protestants who had been protesting violently against Catholicism). Alba's actions led to thousands of Dutch Protestants fleeing into exile, many to England.

Elizabeth I was concerned about Alba's presence in the Netherlands for two reasons.

- Alba's large army, with its mission against Protestantism, was within easy striking distance of England. This especially worried Sir William Cecil.
- Elizabeth did not want to become seen as Europe's leading Protestant monarch. She wished to avoid war and openly condemned the Dutch rebels. Nevertheless the rebels still came to England.

Many Protestants, including those on Elizabeth I's Privy Council, saw events overseas as part of an international struggle between Protestantism (the 'true religion') and Catholicism. There was a belief that Spain, as the greatest Catholic power, wanted to destroy Protestantism everywhere, including England. Elizabeth was therefore coming under increasing pressure to deal with the threat posed by Alba's presence in the Netherlands. However, she wanted to avoid war at all costs. England did not have the resources to take on Spain – or worse, France and Spain together. Also a war fought on the basis of religious differences could threaten England with civil war. Yet at the same time she was also very aware of the dangers posed by Spain's mission in the Netherlands.

Source B

Colour engraving from 1567 showing the Spanish Inquisition arriving in the Netherlands. The Duke of Alba established a Council of Troubles to persecute not only rebels but heretics. Hundreds were killed.

Activity ?

Look at Source B. What impact would pictures such as this have had on Elizabeth I and her Privy Council? Why might they be especially concerned in 1568?

Some Dutch rebels fled by taking to the water. Known as the Sea Beggars, they attacked Spanish ships in the English Channel that were carrying men and resources to Alba's armies in the Netherlands. In 1567, Elizabeth began allowing the Sea Beggars to shelter in English harbours.

In 1568, Spanish ships carrying gold to pay Alba's troops in the Netherlands also took refuge in English ports – from the Sea Beggars. The money was a loan to Philip II from bankers in the Italian city of Genoa. Elizabeth decided to take the gold herself, arguing that since it was a loan it didn't belong to Spain but to the Italian bankers. This event is known as the **Genoese Loan**. These developments greatly angered the Spanish.

What was Elizabeth trying to achieve?

Elizabeth was trying to protect English interests without going to war. By making Spain's task in the Netherlands as difficult as possible, she hoped to encourage Spanish forces to leave and allow the Dutch to continue governing themselves as before. Her strategy of harassing Spain was risky and became riskier still in 1568–69, when the Catholic threat from within England became more serious. Two main factors were the cause of this threat.

1   In 1568, Mary, Queen of Scots, fled to England from Scotland. She had a stronger claim to the throne than Elizabeth I from the point-of-view of many Catholics.

2   In 1569, the Revolt of the Northern Earls had taken place. This was a revolt by senior Catholic, English earls in the north of England (see Chapter 2). There had been hope that some of Alba's troops would land in Hartlepool to support it. Although this had not happened, one of the consequences of the rebellion was to encourage Philip II and the pope to back further plots against Elizabeth I, again with the possibility of using Alba's army to topple the queen.

Activities

1. After reviewing the section 'The nature and extent of the Catholic challenge', draw a line down the centre of a piece of paper. This will be a timeline of Catholic threats to Elizabeth I. On one side of the line put threats from home, and on the other put foreign threats. What do you notice about the Catholic threat to Elizabeth I in the 1560s?

2. Two of the key foreign Catholic challenges to England in the 1560s came from France and the Spanish Netherlands. Which do you think was more of a serious threat to Elizabeth? Explain your reasons.

3. How serious was the Catholic challenge to Elizabeth I in England? Use a value continuum like the one below, starting at 0% (Elizabeth I faced no threat at all) and going up to 100% (Elizabeth I was almost overthrown) to help you decide. The more serious you think the threat was, the higher the score will be. Discuss with a partner, then write a short paragraph explaining your decisions. Use any evidence, facts or figures from this chapter to support your explanation.

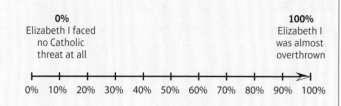

Summary

- Challenges to the religious settlement came from both at home and abroad.
- In England, the Catholic challenge to the religious settlement was limited until 1569.
- The Puritans challenged both the use of crucifixes and vestments.
- Elizabeth sent troops and financial assistance to deal with the Catholic challenge to Protestants in Scotland (1560) and France (1562) but did not do so for the Dutch (1566).
- England's relations with Spain got much worse after the Dutch Revolt began.
- The Dutch Revolt caused concern to England because of the large Spanish army sent to the Netherlands to put it down and crush Protestant heresy.
- By sheltering the Sea Beggars and seizing gold bullion from Philip II's ships, Elizabeth hoped to make it too difficult for Spanish forces to remain in the Netherlands.

Checkpoint

Strengthen

S1 Describe the crucifix and vestments controversies and their outcomes.

S2 Give two reasons why the Catholic threat in England was not serious until 1569.

S3 What was the Dutch Revolt about and why was Spain involved?

S4 Give two reasons why the Dutch Revolt worried Elizabeth so much.

S5 Give two examples of things Elizabeth did that annoyed Spain.

Challenge

C1 Explain why Elizabeth intervened to help Protestants in France but not in the Netherlands.

C2 Explain how developments in England and the Netherlands combined during the 1560s to change England's relationship with Spain.

For these questions, it might be helpful to draw a timeline of events. Having a visual representation of the period may make things clearer when writing your answers.

1.4 The problem of Mary, Queen of Scots

Timeline

Mary, Queen of Scots

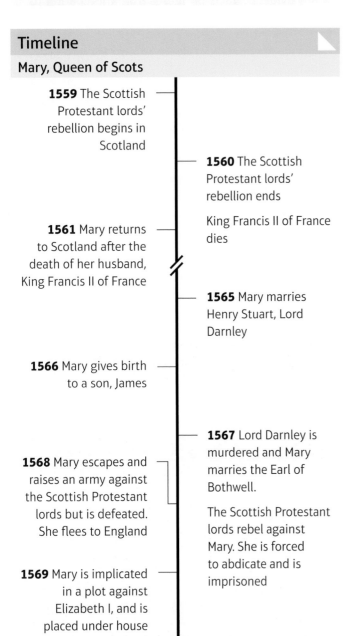

1559 The Scottish Protestant lords' rebellion begins in Scotland

1560 The Scottish Protestant lords' rebellion ends

King Francis II of France dies

1561 Mary returns to Scotland after the death of her husband, King Francis II of France

1565 Mary marries Henry Stuart, Lord Darnley

1566 Mary gives birth to a son, James

1567 Lord Darnley is murdered and Mary marries the Earl of Bothwell.

The Scottish Protestant lords rebel against Mary. She is forced to abdicate and is imprisoned

1568 Mary escapes and raises an army against the Scottish Protestant lords but is defeated. She flees to England

1569 Mary is implicated in a plot against Elizabeth I, and is placed under house arrest in England

Mary, Queen of Scots' claim to the English throne

As noted earlier, Mary, Queen of Scots, was a Catholic with a strong claim to the English throne. She was Henry VII's great granddaughter, Elizabeth I's second cousin, and there were no issues about her legitimacy. Born on 8 December 1542, she became queen of Scotland at six days old after her father, King James V, died. Her mother, Mary of Guise, was from a very powerful Catholic, French noble family.

The Treaty of Edinburgh, 1560

In 1560, Elizabeth I helped Scotland's Protestant lords defeat Mary of Guise, who had been ruling Scotland for her daughter, Mary, Queen of Scots, whilst she was in France with her husband, King Francis II.

The Scottish Protestant lords rebelled because they did not like the French, Catholic influence brought to Scotland by Mary of Guise. Although Elizabeth was wary of sending help to a rebellion which could see the deposing of an anointed* monarch, she was also under constant threat: with French help, Mary, Queen of Scots, could take her throne. With the encouragement of her advisers, Elizabeth secretly sent money to help the rebels, and eventually sent troops, too.

Key term

Anointed*

During a coronation, holy oil is applied to the monarch. This is known as 'anointing' and is the most important part of the coronation as it is when the person becomes the monarch.

The rebellion ended with the Treaty of Edinburgh in 1560. The treaty said that Mary, Queen of Scots, would give up her claim to the English throne. After the unexpected death of her husband, King Francis II of France, in December 1560, Mary returned to Scotland from France. Although she was queen, the Protestant lords controlled the Scottish government.

Mary herself never approved the treaty, and maintained that she had a claim to the English throne. She wanted to be named as Elizabeth's heir.

Elizabeth had no intention of naming any heir, however, and choosing Mary would divide England: she would be popular with Catholics, but not Protestants. Divisions would damage the kingdom and weaken Elizabeth's position.

Extend your knowledge

Decision to help the rebels

Elizabeth was only persuaded to help the Scottish Protestant lords' rebellion in 1560 because Sir William Cecil persuaded her. In fact, he threatened to resign if she didn't. It was important for England to have a friendly, Protestant, anti-French government in Scotland.

Key term

Abdicate*

A king or queen giving up their throne.

Mary, Queen of Scots' arrival in England, 1568

Mary married her second husband, Henry Stuart, Lord Darnley, in 1565. She gave birth to their son, James, in 1566. In 1567, Darnley was murdered, probably by the Earl of Bothwell and Mary was suspected of being involved. In fact, she married Bothwell soon after Darnley's death, which for many was admission of her guilt.

The scandal led to the Protestant Scottish lords rebelling again. They forced Mary to abdicate* in favour of her baby son, James. She was imprisoned in a castle on an island in the middle of a loch (lake), but escaped in 1568 and raised an army in an attempt to win back her throne. Mary's forces were defeated at Langside, near Glasgow, and she fled to England, seeking Elizabeth I's help against the rebels.

Source A

A 16th-century Scottish painting of Mary, Queen of Scots (right), and her husband, Henry Stuart, Lord Darnley. Lord Darnley was Mary's distant cousin and also descended from King Henry VII, so he too had a claim to the English throne.

Relations between Elizabeth and Mary, 1568–69

What were Elizabeth's options?

Mary's arrival in England in May 1568 was a problem to which there was no good solution. Elizabeth did not approve of subjects overthrowing their rightful monarchs, but she was very aware of the potential threat Mary posed to her throne. Mary was held in comfort, but under guard, until Elizabeth decided what to do with her. The options were:

1 help Mary to regain her throne
2 hand Mary over to the Scottish lords
3 allow Mary to go abroad
4 keep Mary in England.

Activities ?

1 Imagine you are Elizabeth I. List the pros and cons of the four options concerning what to do with Mary.

2 If you were Elizabeth I, which option would you choose and why? Write a short letter to your Secretary of State, Sir William Cecil, explaining your decision. To do this, you will need to explain why you rejected the other options.

3 Split into two groups, with one group arguing for Mary being allowed to stay in England, and the other group against. Conduct a debate. Make sure you include all the information you listed in your pros and cons list.

The two queens never met, although they did exchange letters. Mary had asked for a meeting with Elizabeth to persuade her of her innocence in Darnley's murder, but her request was refused.

A court was convened to hear the case against her between October 1568 and January 1569. The Scottish lords brought letters with them apparently proving Mary's guilt. Mary said that the court had no right to try her because she was an anointed monarch and would not offer a plea unless Elizabeth guaranteed a verdict of innocent. Elizabeth refused.

Guilty or not guilty?

No verdict could solve the Mary, Queen of Scots, problem. If found guilty, she would be returned to the rebel Scottish lords as their prisoner, and Elizabeth would have been supporting the deposing of an anointed monarch, who was also her cousin. If found innocent, Mary would be free to raise an army, possibly with foreign Catholic support, which would pose too big a threat to Elizabeth's throne.

The court did not reach any conclusions. Mary therefore stayed in England, in captivity. She remained a threat to Elizabeth, as Interpretation 1 shows.

Interpretation 1

Historian Susan Brigden discusses the threat of Mary, Queen of Scots, in her book, *New Worlds, Lost Worlds* (2000).

Whether in England or in Scotland or in France, Mary posed a perpetual menace, for she always pressed her claim to the English throne, and sought by any means to free herself from a protection which became captivity.

Extend your knowledge

Why not make Mary heir to the throne?

It is often thought that Elizabeth's attitude to Mary, Queen of Scots, and her refusal to name her as heir, is at least partly explained by jealousy. Mary was considered a great beauty.

It is important to remember, however, that Elizabeth was a queen and an intelligent woman who understood politics very well. She was increasingly concerned about both the threat from foreign, Catholic powers and her own Catholic subjects. Naming a Catholic heir could make divisions in England worse, or encourage Catholics to put Mary on the throne instead. Many of her advisers and Privy Councillors were Protestants, and Mary was not popular with them. Naming her the heir to the English throne would increase her status and could damage Elizabeth's position, too.

THINKING HISTORICALLY   Cause and Consequence (4a&b)

Fragile history

Nothing that happens is inevitable. Sometimes things happen due to the actions of an individual or chance events that no one anticipated. Something could have altered or someone could have chosen differently, bringing about a very different outcome. What actually occurred in the past did happen, but it did not have to be like that.

Work on your own and answer the questions below. When you have answered the questions, discuss the answers in a group. Then have a class vote.

Perceived reasons why Elizabeth I successfully established her religious settlement

Elizabeth I's middle way strategy, acceptable to both Catholics and Protestants	Growth of Protestantism in England	Recusants were not treated harshly	Visitations to enforce Elizabeth's religious settlement	The decision to keep Mary, Queen of Scots in captivity in England	Catholic Spain and France did not unite against Protestant England	Elizabeth I not getting directly involved in the Dutch Revolt

1   Consider Elizabeth I's middle way strategy.

   a How did not treating recusants harshly affect the success of Elizabeth I's middle way strategy?

   b Had recusants been treated harshly, would the middle way strategy be relevant?

2   Consider Elizabeth's motivations.

   a What might have happened if Elizabeth I had decided to take military action to support the Dutch rebels?

   b Would all the other causes still be relevant?

   c What might have happened if Spain and France had united against England?

   d How did keeping Mary, Queen of Scots in captivity in England affect the outcome?

3   Write down any reasons why the Elizabethan religious settlement was successful that could be called 'chance events'. How important were these in the success of the Elizabethan religious settlement?

4   Imagine you are alive in November 1558, when Elizabeth I became Protestant queen of a country that was still basically Roman Catholic. Write a paragraph explaining whether you think Elizabeth I will be able to establish her religion in England over the next 11 years. Remember not to use the benefit of hindsight!

5   Have a class vote. Was the success of Elizabeth I's religious settlement inevitable? Be prepared to back up your decision.

Exam-style question, Section B

Explain why the Catholic threat to Elizabeth I increased after 1566.

You may use the following in your answer:

• The Dutch Revolt

• Mary, Queen of Scots' arrival in England in 1568.

You must also use information of your own.   **12 marks**

Exam tip

Don't just describe events. You must focus on reasons for the Catholic threat against Elizabeth becoming more serious.

Activity ?

Create a spider diagram showing the reasons why Elizabeth was so cautious when making a decision about the fate of Mary, Queen of Scots.

Plot and rebellion, 1569

Not only would Elizabeth not name an heir, she refused to discuss marriage either. In 1569, a plot was hatched at court that seemed not only to deal with the problem of Mary, but also the succession. The plan was to marry Mary to the Duke of Norfolk, England's most senior noble. He was a Protestant so any children would be too. They would also have a strong claim to the throne. Mary liked the plot. Even some of Elizabeth's favourites, like the Earl of Leicester, were involved – at first. As the plan developed, however, he changed his mind.

The Earl of Leicester eventually told Elizabeth of the plan. It confirmed how dangerous Mary was, even in captivity. She was moved south to Coventry. Nevertheless, Elizabeth still refused to take any strong action against Mary.

Summary

- Mary, Queen of Scots (Elizabeth's second cousin), is **NOT** Queen Mary I (Elizabeth's sister).
- Mary, Queen of Scots' arrival in England was a huge problem for Elizabeth I.
- Mary had a strong claim to be next in line to the English throne after Elizabeth.
- Mary became the focus of a plot at court in 1569 to marry her to the Duke of Norfolk.
- The plot to marry Mary to the Duke of Norfolk was developed into a rebellion by the Catholic earls of Northumberland and Westmorland.
- Elizabeth did not want to take action against Mary because she was an anointed monarch.
- From 1568, Mary remained in captivity in England.

Checkpoint

Strengthen

S1 Describe the chain of events that led Mary, Queen of Scots, to come to England.

S2 Give two options Elizabeth had in dealing with Mary and say why she did not take them.

S3 What was the aim of the plot concerning Mary that developed at court?

Challenge

C1 Explain how changes in Scotland and France caused problems for Elizabeth I.

C2 Explain why there was no ideal solution to the Mary problem for Elizabeth I, including holding her in captivity in England.

If you are not confident about constructing answers to these questions, write a list of all factors related to the problems described, using information from the chapter to help you. This will help to structure your answer.

Recap: Queen, government and religion, 1558–69

Recall quiz

1. What were the key features of the Privy Council?
2. What were the three key parts of Elizabeth's religious settlement?
3. Give two ways in which the religious settlement was enforced.
4. Which parts of England had the most Catholic support during Elizabeth's early reign?
5. Give three pieces of evidence that show the religious settlement wasn't accepted by everyone.
6. In what year did the Dutch Revolt begin?
7. Which treaty was signed in 1560? What was the main aim of the treaty?
8. Who was Mary, Queen of Scots, accused of murdering?
9. Give two reasons why Elizabeth needed to keep Mary, Queen of Scots, in captivity.
10. Who plotted to become Mary, Queen of Scots' husband?

Exam-style question, Section B

'Religion was Elizabeth's main problem in the years 1558-69'. How far do you agree? Explain your answer.

You may use the following in your answer:

- the settlement of religion
- Mary, Queen of Scots' arrival in England in 1568.

You must also use information of your own **16 marks**

Exam tip

This question is asking you to assess the significance of many different factors and come to a conclusion of which was the most important. You will need to discuss problems other than religion in your answer. Remember to come to a conclusion at the end of your answer which summarises all your points and makes a judgement about the statement.

Activities

1. Write Elizabeth I's report card. How successful was Elizabeth's first decade of rule?

This will come in three sections:

   a The Settlement of Religion
   b Religious Challenges
   c The problem of Mary, Queen of Scots.

In pairs, for each of these sections, work out what you think Elizabeth I's aims were. Then get together with another pair and compare your lists. Add any aims you are missing.

Now for each section you must give Elizabeth a score on the following scale:

   1 = Complete failure. No aims met.
   2 = Largely a failure. Majority of aims not met.
   3 = Largely a success. Majority of aims met.
   4 = Complete success. All aims met.

Under each heading, write the score you are giving Elizabeth and a short assessment of her performance. To do this, you should explain which of her aims were met and which weren't by referring to key events and outcomes.

   d Draw up a list of Elizabeth's strengths and weaknesses in 1569. How do they compare with the lists you drew up for the activity on page 14? Now identify her opportunities and threats.

   e What do you see as Elizabeth's greatest threat in the decade to come? Explain your decision.

   f What do you see as Elizabeth's greatest opportunity? Explain your decision.

Writing historically: managing sentences

Successful historical writing is clearly expressed, using carefully managed sentence structures.

Learning outcomes

By the end of this lesson, you will understand how to:

- select and use single clause and multiple clause sentences.

Definitions

Clause: a group of words, or unit of meaning, that contains a verb, and can form part or all of a sentence, e.g. 'Elizabeth I reigned over England from 1558'.

Single clause sentence: a sentence containing just one clause, e.g. 'Elizabeth I reigned over England from 1558.'

Multiple clause sentence: a sentence containing two or more clauses, often linked with a conjunction, e.g. 'Elizabeth I reigned over England from 1558 and was known as 'The Virgin Queen'.'

Co-ordinating conjunction: a word used to link two clauses of equal importance within a sentence, e.g. 'and', 'but', 'so', 'or', etc.

How can I structure my sentences clearly?

When you are explaining and exploring complex events and ideas, you can end up writing very long sentences. These can make your writing difficult for the reader to follow.

Look at the extract below from a response to this exam-style question:

> Describe **two** features of the Revolt of the Northern Earls. **(4 marks)**

> England was a Protestant country but the Northern Earls and their followers aimed to bring back Catholicism in England so they began a revolt and at the beginning of the revolt they took control of Durham Cathedral and celebrated mass there.

1. The writer of the response above has linked every piece of information in his answer into one, very long sentence.

   How many different pieces of information has the writer included in this answer? Rewrite each piece of information as a **single clause sentence**. For example:

   > The Northern Earls wanted England to be Catholic.

2. Look again at your answer to question 1. Which of the single clause sentences would you link together? Rewrite the response twice, experimenting with linking different sentences together using **conjunctions** such as 'and', 'but' or 'so'. Remember: you are aiming to make your writing as clear and precise as possible.

3. Now write a paragraph in response to the exam-style question below, using only single clause sentences to state each different piece of information.

   > Describe **two** features of Elizabethan government in 1558. **(4 marks)**

4. Now rewrite your response to Question 3. Experiment with linking different sentences together using conjunctions such as 'and', 'but' or 'so'. Remember: you are aiming to make your writing as clear and precise as possible.

How can I use conjunctions to link my ideas?

There are several types of **multiple clause sentence** structures that you can use to link your ideas.

If you want to balance or contrast two ideas of equal importance within a sentence, you can use co-ordinating conjunctions to link them.

Look at the extract below from a response to this exam-style question:

> Explain why the Catholic threat to Elizabeth I increased after 1566.
>
> **(12 marks)**

> *Mary, Queen of Scots, arrived in England in 1568. Because she was a Catholic and had a link to the English throne, with the support of France, many saw her as a Catholic alternative to Elizabeth. This* not only *worried Elizabeth,* but also *gave many the chance to plot against her whilst Mary was close by. Mary continuously pressed her claim for the English throne,* not face *to face with Elizabeth* but *through letters, as Elizabeth refused to meet her in person.*

These co-ordinating conjunctions link equally important actions that happened at the same time.

These paired co-ordinating conjunctions contrast two different means of communication.

These paired co-ordinating conjunctions link and balance two equally important ideas.

5. How else could the writer of the response above have linked, balanced or contrasted these ideas? Experiment with rewriting the response, using different sentence structures and different ways of linking ideas within them.

Did you notice?

The first sentence in the response above is a single clause sentence:

> *Mary, Queen of Scots, arrived in England in 1568.*

6. Why do you think the writer chose to give this point additional emphasis by structuring it as a short, single clause sentence? Write a sentence or two explaining your ideas.

Improving an answer

7. Now look at the final paragraph below, which shows the response to the exam-style question above.

> *After 1566, Elizabeth faced threats from many different Catholic foes. Mary, Queen of Scots, served as a constant reminder that she was a Catholic alternative to the Protestant Elizabeth. With this threat so close to home, plots were easily hatched. The Revolt of the Northern Earls was not a revolt of ordinary Elizabethan people. Many high-ranking members of the nobility were involved. Elizabeth could not underestimate these Catholic threats.*

Rewrite this paragraph, choosing some conjunctions from the **Co-ordinating Conjunction Bank** below to link, balance or contrast the writer's ideas.

Co-ordinating Conjunction Bank	
and	not only… but also…
but	either… or…
or	neither… nor…
so	both… and…

02 | Challenges to Elizabeth at home and abroad, 1569–88

Elizabeth I faced many serious threats between 1569 and 1588, both from within England and from abroad. These threats were often linked.

In northern England, Elizabeth faced threats from members of the nobility who, increasingly sympathetic to Mary, Queen of Scots and her Catholic cause, revolted in 1569. Elizabeth faced many other plots against her rule (and her life) during this time.

Elsewhere, England's failing relationship with Spain prompted Philip II of Spain to offer support to English Catholics plotting to remove the Protestant Elizabeth from the English throne. Roman Catholic priests were smuggled in from Europe to keep the Catholic faith in England alive, resulting in more plots being hatched against the Protestant queen on English soil.

The rivalry between England and Spain was not just based on religion, but also trade and political power. In Europe, England's increasing involvement in the Netherlands angered Philip II, as the Netherlands was under Spanish rule.

Philip also ruled a large and expanding empire. Europeans had only been aware of the Americas, known as the 'New World', since 1492. By the time of Elizabeth's reign, Spain had established colonies, religious missions and trading outposts there. Sir Francis Drake, and others like him, did what they could to disrupt Spain's interests and establish English colonies in the New World, often resorting to attacking and robbing Spanish ships. Elizabeth backed and rewarded Drake for his efforts.

By the mid-1580s, England and Spain were at war, despite Elizabeth's efforts to avoid a conflict. Philip planned an invasion of England, and in 1588 he launched his Armada.

Learning outcomes

By the end of this chapter, you will:

- understand the plots against Elizabeth I and know how the Elizabethan government was able to monitor threats to the queen
- know and understand the key events in the decline in Anglo–Spanish relations, 1569–88
- understand why Mary was finally executed in 1587
- understand why events in the Netherlands were so important to the security of England
- understand why Philip II sent the Armada against England in 1588 and why it failed.

2.1 Plots and revolts at home

Learning objectives

- Understand the key points of the Revolt of the Northern Earls, including why they rebelled, the key players, and role of religion and politics.
- Understand the significance of the Ridolfi, Throckmorton and Babington plots.
- Understand the significance of Mary, Queen of Scots' execution.
- Know how Walsingham used spies.

By the end of the 1560s Elizabeth I faced a range of threats to her throne, both at home and from abroad. These threats culminated in Philip II sending the Spanish Armada to invade England in 1588. He hoped that English Catholics would rise up and join his forces in deposing Elizabeth I. Philip believed that the many plots against Elizabeth were a sign of civil unrest in England. Figure 2.1 highlights the main threats Elizabeth faced at the beginning of the 1570s.

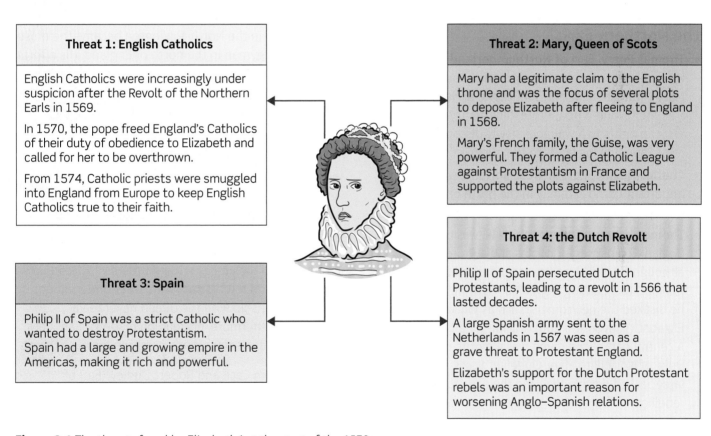

Threat 1: English Catholics

English Catholics were increasingly under suspicion after the Revolt of the Northern Earls in 1569.

In 1570, the pope freed England's Catholics of their duty of obedience to Elizabeth and called for her to be overthrown.

From 1574, Catholic priests were smuggled into England from Europe to keep English Catholics true to their faith.

Threat 2: Mary, Queen of Scots

Mary had a legitimate claim to the English throne and was the focus of several plots to depose Elizabeth after fleeing to England in 1568.

Mary's French family, the Guise, was very powerful. They formed a Catholic League against Protestantism in France and supported the plots against Elizabeth.

Threat 3: Spain

Philip II of Spain was a strict Catholic who wanted to destroy Protestantism.
Spain had a large and growing empire in the Americas, making it rich and powerful.

Threat 4: the Dutch Revolt

Philip II of Spain persecuted Dutch Protestants, leading to a revolt in 1566 that lasted decades.

A large Spanish army sent to the Netherlands in 1567 was seen as a grave threat to Protestant England.

Elizabeth's support for the Dutch Protestant rebels was an important reason for worsening Anglo–Spanish relations.

Figure 2.1 The threats faced by Elizabeth I at the start of the 1570s.

The Revolt of the Northern Earls, 1569

The north of England was far away from London, and therefore Elizabeth I and her court. The majority of people living in the north of England remained loyal to the old religion, Catholicism, and the ancient noble families who had governed the north for centuries. Both came under threat during Elizabeth I's reign: she introduced Protestantism and promoted 'new men' from the gentry and lower ranks of the nobility to some of the most important government positions. In 1569, Elizabeth faced a serious threat when some northern earls led Catholic northerners against her.

Why did the northern earls revolt in 1569?

Several factors came together which led to the Revolt of the Northern Earls in 1569.

- The earls and their followers wanted Catholicism restored in England.
- The earls had lost a great deal of their influence at court since Elizabeth I became queen in 1558.
- Elizabeth refused to name an heir or to marry and have a child, creating uncertainty about England's future.
- Mary, Queen of Scots, in captivity in England, was a figurehead who could potentially replace Elizabeth and, in doing so, resolve the other issues the earls had.

Who were the key players in the Revolt of the Northern Earls?

- **Thomas Percy, Earl of Northumberland** was Catholic. He had held an important position at court under Mary I, but lost a lot of his influence under Elizabeth I, as she favoured new, Protestant gentry. He had also lost the rights to a valuable, newly discovered copper mine found on his lands to the queen in 1567.
- **Charles Neville, Earl of Westmorland**, was from an important Catholic family in the north of England. He was also the Duke of Norfolk's brother-in-law.
- **Thomas Howard, Duke of Norfolk**, was one of England's most senior nobles and a Protestant, although he had close links to old, northern Catholic families, too. Coming from an ancient noble family, he disliked the newcomers, such as William Cecil and Elizabeth's favourite, Robert Dudley, Earl of Leicester. A central part of the revolt was a plot to marry the Duke of Norfolk to Mary, Queen of Scots. However, he later backed down and urged the earls to call off the rebellion.
- **Mary, Queen of Scots**, had met the Duke of Norfolk once, shortly after fleeing to England from Scotland in 1568. She supported the plan to marry him and perhaps even take the English throne.
- **Jane Neville** was the wife of Charles Neville and the Duke of Norfolk's sister. She was key in encouraging her husband to carry on with the rebellion. If the rebellion succeeded, she could be sister-in-law to the queen of England.
- **Ann Percy**, the wife of Thomas Percy, was also key in encouraging her husband in the rebellion.

Activity   ?

Study the profiles of the key players in the Revolt of the Northern Earls. How many different reasons can you find to explain why they would want to rebel?

What role did religion play?

Much of the north of England, including the earls of Northumberland and Westmorland, held on to traditional Roman Catholic beliefs, despite Elizabeth's religious settlement in 1559. Although she did not want to persecute Catholics, Elizabeth did want their religion to die out eventually. She appointed James Pilkington, a committed Protestant, as archbishop of Durham in 1561. By doing this, Elizabeth hoped to lessen the influence of Catholicism in the North. Pilkington became the most important clergyman in the north of England. His efforts to impose Protestantism were very unpopular, however, and only succeeded in turning many northerners against him and against England's new religion.

What role did politics play?

Under Mary I, the Catholic earls of Northumberland and Westmorland had been very influential, both at court and locally in the north of England. Northumberland resented an up-and-coming rival northern family, the Forsters. Elizabeth I favoured Sir John Forster and gave him the task of looking after the borders with Scotland. Northumberland felt his own status was undermined and his relationship with the queen never really recovered. Furthermore, his religion made William Cecil (one of the queen's closest advisers) see him as a threat.

Men like William Cecil and Robert Dudley (Earl of Leicester) did not come from ancient noble families such as the Percys and Nevilles, but were very close to the queen. The northern earls resented these newcomers, and the influence they had over Elizabeth.

Mary, Queen of Scots, and the succession

Elizabeth I refused to name an heir. It was becoming clear that she had no desire to marry, and so would not give birth to the next king or queen.

If she were to die before she declared an heir to the throne, England could be thrown into confusion – possibly even civil war*.

Mary, Queen of Scots, had a strong claim to the English throne. The Revolt of the Northern Earls started as a wider court conspiracy* for her to marry the Duke of Norfolk, which meant many people at the court of Elizabeth knew of the plot. The marriage would solve the problem of what to do about Mary, and any children they had would provide heirs. Even though Mary was Catholic, Norfolk was Protestant and Elizabeth's courtiers assumed his heirs would be, too. With this in mind, some believed that if Mary married the Duke of Norfolk and Elizabeth named her as her heir, England would still have a Protestant monarch on Elizabeth's death.

Although the conspiracy to marry the Duke of Norfolk was not treason, as it developed some of Elizabeth's courtiers got cold feet for several reasons.

- The marriage of members of the nobility required the queen's consent.
- Elizabeth I had made it clear that the succession was a matter of royal prerogative.
- The Duke of Norfolk was sympathetic to Catholics and close to the Catholic earls of Northumberland and Westmorland, for whom Mary, Queen of Scots, would be a preferable monarch.

Key terms

Civil war*

A war between people of the same country.

Conspiracy*

A secret plan with the aim of doing something against the law.

Furthermore, Source A shows that Mary's motives were already more ambitious than just marrying Norfolk. It also shows that the Spanish ambassador to Elizabeth's court was involved in the plot. In fact, Mary had received word that Spain would provide troops to help with the rebellion.

Source A

A letter to Philip II written by Guerau de Spes, Spain's ambassador to Elizabeth's court, on 8 January 1569.

The Queen of Scotland told my servant to convey to me the following words: – 'Tell the ambassador that, if his master will help me, I shall be Queen of England in three months and mass shall be said all over the country'.

Eventually, in September 1569, Robert Dudley, the Earl of Leicester, decided to inform Elizabeth I of the plot. By this time, it was far more developed than simply marrying Norfolk to Mary, as shown in Figure 2.2.

Plan for the Revolt of the Northern Earls, November–December, 1569

1. *The earls of Northumberland and Westmorland will raise rebel forces from their lands in the north of England and take control of Durham.*

2. *The rebels will then march south towards London to join with the Duke of Norfolk.*

3. *Several thousand Spanish troops will land in Hartlepool to support the rebel forces.*

4. *The Duke of Norfolk and the rebel forces will seize control of the government in London and overthrow Elizabeth I.*

5. *Any resistance will be overthrown by the Spanish troops.*

6. *Meanwhile, Mary, Queen of Scots, is to be freed, ready to marry the Duke of Norfolk and take the English throne.*

Figure 2.2 The plans made by northern earls for their revolt, 1569.

The key events of the revolt

Once Elizabeth knew about the plot, Norfolk was arrested. He was sent to the Tower of London on 1 November 1569. When they heard the news, the earls of Northumberland and Westmorland became desperate and, with their wives' support and urging, pushed ahead with the revolt. Heading for Durham, they took control of the cathedral from James Pilkington, who fled south. They destroyed any evidence of Protestantism and celebrated mass. In fact, mass was celebrated at churches across the north-east of England over the next fortnight.

The rebels then turned south, bearing banners with religious symbols. Mary, Queen of Scots, was moved south to Coventry on the orders of Elizabeth. Elizabeth did not want Mary to escape.

The rebellion ultimately failed: Spain's supporting troops never arrived and Elizabeth managed to raise an army of 14,000 men for her cause. However, as Figure 2.3 shows, the rebellion presented a real threat to Elizabeth.

After the revolt was crushed, approximately 450 rebels were executed throughout the towns and villages of northern England on Elizabeth's orders, with the aim of terrifying the population and preventing another rebellion. Westmorland escaped, but Northumberland was captured. He was executed in York in 1572, and his head was put on a spike above the city's gates. The Privy Council called for Norfolk's execution, too; however, Elizabeth released him. Meanwhile, Mary, Queen of Scots, remained in captivity for the next 14 years.

Although Elizabeth I acted harshly against many of the rebels, she hesitated when it came to the Duke of Norfolk and especially Mary, Queen of Scots. The Scots had overthrown their rightful queen and executing Mary would imply that Elizabeth accepted what they had done. Being an anointed monarch made you God's chosen ruler and subjects did not have the right to change that. However, Elizabeth's reluctance to deal with Mary frustrated her Privy Council and parliament, and the situation was also exploited by others: it was not long before another plot involving Mary was hatched.

The failed revolt led the pope to take action against Elizabeth I. In 1570, he issued a papal bull* that excommunicated Elizabeth and called on all loyal

> ### Key term
>
> **Papal bull***
> A written order issued by the pope.

> ### Activity ?
>
> Study Figure 2.3. Which three points in the revolt do you think would have given Elizabeth I most cause for concern? Why?

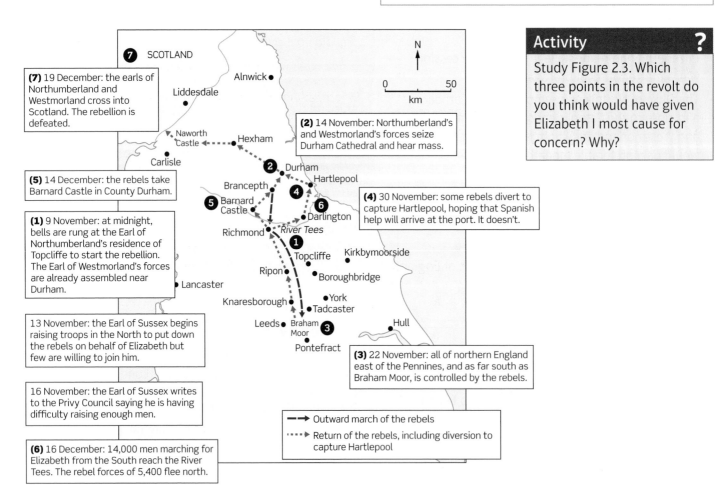

(7) 19 December: the earls of Northumberland and Westmorland cross into Scotland. The rebellion is defeated.

(2) 14 November: Northumberland's and Westmorland's forces seize Durham Cathedral and hear mass.

(5) 14 December: the rebels take Barnard Castle in County Durham.

(4) 30 November: some rebels divert to capture Hartlepool, hoping that Spanish help will arrive at the port. It doesn't.

(1) 9 November: at midnight, bells are rung at the Earl of Northumberland's residence of Topcliffe to start the rebellion. The Earl of Westmorland's forces are already assembled near Durham.

13 November: the Earl of Sussex begins raising troops in the North to put down the rebels on behalf of Elizabeth but few are willing to join him.

16 November: the Earl of Sussex writes to the Privy Council saying he is having difficulty raising enough men.

(6) 16 December: 14,000 men marching for Elizabeth from the South reach the River Tees. The rebel forces of 5,400 flee north.

(3) 22 November: all of northern England east of the Pennines, and as far south as Braham Moor, is controlled by the rebels.

→ Outward march of the rebels
┈┈▶ Return of the rebels, including diversion to capture Hartlepool

Figure 2.3 The Revolt of the Northern Earls, 1569.

Catholics to depose her, hoping that it would encourage another rebellion. Elizabeth struck back. She called for parliament to assemble. In April 1571, parliament passed Acts widening the definition of treason. It became treasonable to claim that Elizabeth I was a heretic, was not the queen and also to bring in, or print, papal bulls in England.

The significance of the Revolt of the Northern Earls

- It was the first, and most serious, rebellious act by English Catholics against Elizabeth I.

- The treason laws became harsher and the definition of treason was widened.

- It ended the power and influence of the Percy and Neville families in the north of England.

- It prompted harsher treatment of Catholics. For example, in 1572, Elizabeth sent the Earl of Huntingdon, a committed Protestant, to lead the Council of the North*. He implemented laws against Catholics and effectively suppressed Catholicism.

- Although Elizabeth's brutal revenge on the executed rebels indicates how seriously she saw the threat of the revolt to her rule, the majority of Catholics in northern England remained loyal. However, the revolt encouraged the pope, Pius V, to excommunicate Elizabeth I. His papal bull marked a turning point for English Catholics: their loyalty to Elizabeth was now always in doubt.

Key term

Council of the North*

The Council of the North was used to implement Elizabeth's laws and authority in the north of England, as it was far from London and Elizabeth's reach. The North was sometimes unstable and often under threat from Scottish raids. It was therefore necessary to have a Council with special powers that could take action in times of lawlessness and emergency.

The significance of the papal bull

The papal bull issued by the pope put England's Catholics in a difficult position: did they obey the head of their church or their queen? Now that a direct order had been issued by the pope, loyalty to both their spiritual and political leader was no longer possible, and so doubt was cast over the loyalty of all English Catholics.

The Ridolfi, Throckmorton and Babington plots

The Ridolfi plot, 1571

Roberto Ridolfi was an Italian banker from Florence living in England. He was also one of the pope's spies. In 1571, he arranged a plot to murder Elizabeth, launch a Spanish invasion and put Mary, Queen of Scots, on the throne. As with the Revolt of the Northern Earls, the plan was for Mary to be married to the Duke of Norfolk.

In March 1571, Ridolfi left England to discuss the plot with the pope, Philip II and the Duke of Alba, who was stationed in the Netherlands, a country under Spanish rule. Ridolfi had a letter signed by the Duke of Norfolk declaring he was Catholic and would lead the rebellion if Philip II would support it. Philip II told Alba to prepare 10,000 men to send to England if necessary. Sir William Cecil uncovered the plot and by autumn 1571 he had enough evidence (letters in code), to prove that Norfolk was guilty of plotting against Elizabeth I again. This was high treason. Ridolfi was abroad when his plot was uncovered and never returned to England.

When parliament met again in May 1572, it demanded the execution of both Norfolk and Mary. Elizabeth signed Norfolk's death warrant and he was executed in June 1572. However, Elizabeth would still not take action against Mary, even refusing to bar her from the succession.

Ridolfi's significance

- Coming so soon after the papal bull excommunicating Elizabeth, the Ridolfi plot reinforced the threat posed by Mary and Catholics, both at home and abroad.

- It also reinforced the threat to England from Spain. Already concerned by the Duke of Alba's presence in the Netherlands (as the persecution of Dutch Protestants was becoming more widespread) anxiety about Spain's intentions towards Elizabeth increased.

- Because of the threat from Spain, Elizabeth focused on improving relations with France.

Priests and priest holes

In order to keep Catholicism alive in England and strengthen English Catholics' resistance to Elizabeth and her Protestant Church, Catholic priests were smuggled into England from 1574. They travelled undercover, staying with well-to-do Catholic families, celebrating mass and hearing confessions. This was highly dangerous. Government agents increasingly kept English Catholics under surveillance. Homes where priests were suspected to be staying were raided. Those priests caught risked being hanged, drawn and quartered*, although not all were. In many homes, secret hiding places called priest holes were made. Source B describes a raid on a Catholic house.

Key term

Hanged, drawn and quartered*

A type of punishment used when the accused was found guilty of high treason. The accused would be hanged until near dead, cut open, have their intestines removed, and were finally chopped into four pieces.

Source B

A raid on a Catholic house in Northamptonshire, described by a Catholic priest, John Gerard, who was staying there. He managed to hide in the priest hole without being caught.

There they were, straining and shouting to get through and search the house, yet they halted in an unlocked room just long enough to allow us to reach the hiding-place and shut ourselves safely in. Then they… burst into the lady's apartment while others raged round the remaining rooms.

In 1581, parliament passed two laws against Catholics.

- Recusants would now be fined £20 – an enormous sum that would bankrupt most families.
- Attempting to convert people to Catholicism was now treason.

Measures against English Catholics were becoming harsh, but the plots against Elizabeth continued.

The Throckmorton plot, 1583

The Throckmorton plot planned for the French Duke of Guise, the cousin of Mary, Queen of Scots, to invade England, free Mary, overthrow Elizabeth and restore Catholicism in England. Philip II would provide financial support. A young Englishman, Francis Throckmorton, was to act as a go-between with Mary. The pope also knew, and approved, of the plans.

Sir Francis Walsingham, Elizabeth's Secretary of State from 1573, uncovered the plot. His agents found incriminating papers at Throckmorton's house. Throckmorton was arrested in November 1583, tortured, confessed, and was executed in May 1584. The Throckmorton plot again emphasised the threat of foreign, Catholic powers, English Catholics and Mary, Queen of Scots. It also showed the potential threat if the forces of Spain and France were to combine in future.

Throckmorton's significance

- Throckmorton's papers included a list of Catholic sympathisers in England, suggesting that the government's fear of English Catholics as 'the enemy within' was real.
- Life became harder for Catholics and they were treated with great suspicion by the government. Many important Catholics fled England after the plot, and up to 11,000 were imprisoned or kept under surveillance or house arrest. Another Act of Parliament was passed in 1585 that made helping or sheltering Catholic priests punishable with death.

The Babington plot, 1586

The Babington plot once again centred on the murder of Elizabeth I, and also encouraged English Catholics to rebel. It was similar to the Throckmorton plot: the Duke of Guise would invade England with 60,000 men and put Mary on the throne. Both Philip II of Spain and the pope supported this plot.

Anthony Babington, a Catholic with links to the French, wrote to Mary, Queen of Scots, in July 1586 about the proposed plot. However, Mary was being closely watched and her letters were being intercepted and read by Sir Francis Walsingham. Once he had sufficient details about the plot, including the names of six Catholics prepared to assassinate Elizabeth, all involved were arrested.

Babington and his accomplices were convicted and hanged, drawn and quartered. In October 1586, Mary was finally tried by the Privy Council. There had now been too many plots surrounding her to believe she was innocent of any wrongdoing. Found guilty, she was sentenced to death. Elizabeth, again hesitating, did not sign the warrant for Mary's death until February 1587. The sentence was carried out on 8 February.

Babington's significance

- This plot was especially significant because, by 1585, relations between England and Spain had broken down and the English were aiding the Dutch Protestants in a rebellion against the Spanish. Thus Elizabeth's situation was even more dangerous than had been the case with previous plots.
- Elizabeth's government became determined to crush Catholicism. There were mass arrests of recusants in England, with over 300 in north London alone and 31 priests were executed.
- Mary's execution ended any hope of replacing Elizabeth with a Catholic heir.

Exam-style question, section B ⚪

Describe **two** features of the plots against Elizabeth I in the years 1571–86. **4 marks**

Exam tip ⚪

This question is worth only 4 out of a possible 32 marks. Although 4 marks can make a difference to your overall result, you should only spend about 4–6 minutes on it. This means you must be very clear and concise.

Mary, Queen of Scots' execution

Why was Mary, Queen of Scots, executed?

Mary, Queen of Scots, had been involved in plots before, so why was she executed in 1587? The answer lies partly in a new Act of Parliament that had been passed in 1585: the Act for the Preservation of the Queen's Safety.

The act stated that, in the event of Elizabeth's assassination, Mary, Queen of Scots, was to be barred from the succession. Also, any action against Mary, Queen of Scots should only be taken once a commission has investigated her role in the plot, held a trial and found her guilty.

Source C ◥

Painted c1613. The execution of Mary, Queen of Scots, at Fotheringhay Castle on 8 February 1587.

The evidence gathered by Walsingham against Mary, Queen of Scots, was enough to ensure her trial and conviction in October 1586 under the Act for the Preservation of the Queen's Safety. Elizabeth I finally, but reluctantly, signed her death warrant in February 1587.

Another reason why Mary, Queen of Scots, was executed was that by the start of 1587, it was clear to Elizabeth and her Privy Council that Philip II was planning a major attack against England. In January 1587, there were rumours that Spanish troops had landed in Wales and that Mary had escaped. These rumours reinforced the threat Mary's continued existence posed to England.

What was the significance of Mary, Queen of Scots' execution?

- The execution of Mary, Queen of Scots, removed an important threat to Elizabeth I.
- Philip II had been planning to invade England since 1585. The execution of Mary gave him one more reason to remove Elizabeth from the English throne. Mary also left her claim to the English throne to Philip II upon her death.

Activity **?**

Review the plots against Elizabeth I. Draw and fill in a table with five columns: **Plot name and date**; **Context** (recent events); **Who was involved?**; **The basic plan**; and **Outcomes**.

Walsingham's use of spies

In 1573, Sir Francis Walsingham became Elizabeth I's Secretary of State. In this role, he developed a network of spies and informers, both in England and abroad. He played a crucial role in uncovering plots against Elizabeth I.

Walsingham's spy network

The extent of Walsingham's spy network was impressive. Throughout England, Walsingham had a range of spies and informants in every county and important town. Some were specially trained agents, but many were ordinary people who were paid for useful information. This turned ordinary people into spies on their neighbours. By 1580, Walsingham also had agents in 12 towns in France, nine in Germany, four in Spain, three in Italy and others in Algiers, Tripoli and Istanbul. Walsingham also used ciphers* in written communications to hide his plans to catch those plotting against Elizabeth.

Another source of informants were those few Catholic priests captured after having been smuggled into England, such as John Hart. Held in the Tower in 1581, he offered his services as a spy in return for a pardon. Given that in 1580, at least six priests had been arrested, taken to the Tower, tortured, convicted and executed, Hart's decision is not surprising. Walsingham also used *agents provocateurs** to plot and discover traitors. No one was above suspicion and even members of the nobility were routinely spied upon.

Key terms

Cipher*
A secret way of writing in code.

*Agents provocateurs**
French term referring to agents who become a part of groups suspected of wrongdoing, and encourage other members to break the law so that potential threats can be identified and arrested.

Walsingham did not approve of torture being used against Catholic priests caught in England. He believed it would make people sympathetic towards them. Evidence suggests he only used torture in the most serious of cases, but Source D also gives an interesting insight into Walsingham.

Source D

Sir Francis Walsingham in a letter to Lord Burghley (William Cecil) in 1575. He was writing about trying to stop the plots surrounding Mary, Queen of Scots.

Without torture I know we shall not prevail.

Not all priests who were captured were executed. A special prison was built for them and the conditions were not harsh. Nevertheless, during Elizabeth I's reign, 130 priests and 60 of their supporters were executed.

Activity **?**

Work in pairs. Discuss the following statement: 'Francis Walsingham is one of England's unknown heroes.'

- **a** One person is to list evidence for this statement and the other against. Write up your evidence together in one paragraph. The aim is to produce a persuasive argument.

- **b** Join with another pair. Each person is to read out their argument and listen carefully to everyone else's. Take a vote on whether you agree with the statement or not.

THINKING HISTORICALLY   Cause and Consequence (3a&b)

The might of human agency

1 'Our lack of control'. Work in pairs.

Describe to your partner a situation where things did not work out as you had intended. Then explain how you would have done things differently to make the situation as you would have wanted. Your partner will then tell the group about that situation and whether they think that your alternative actions would have had the desired effect.

2 'The tyranny of failed actions'. Work individually.

The Duke of Norfolk's plans to marry Mary, Queen of Scots in 1569

a Write down what the Duke of Norfolk's aims were.

b Write down what the Duke of Norfolk's actions were.

c To what extent were the Duke of Norfolk's actions successful in achieving their aims?

d Make a spider diagram: write the Duke of Norfolk's actions in the middle and then add as many consequences of his actions as possible around them. Think about the long-term consequences as well as the immediate ones.

e How important were the consequences of the Duke of Norfolk's actions for the future lives of English Catholics?

3 To what extent are historical individuals in control of the history they helped to create? Explain your answer in a paragraph, with reference to specific historical examples from this topic and others you have studied.

Summary

- The Revolt of the Northern Earls in 1569 was a serious rebellion focused on overthrowing Elizabeth I and restoring Catholicism.
- Elizabeth I's excommunication in 1570 put English Catholics in a difficult position between loyalty to their political leader, Elizabeth I, or their spiritual leader, the pope.
- Plots against Elizabeth were encouraged by Spain and the pope.
- Three other plots aiming to replace Elizabeth I with Mary, Queen of Scots, were Ridolfi (1571); Throckmorton (1583); and Babington (1586).
- Mary, Queen of Scots, was executed in 1587 after the Babington Plot.
- Plots against Elizabeth failed because Sir Francis Walsingham had an extensive network of spies and informers.
- Catholic priests were smuggled into England to support English Catholics.

Checkpoint

Strengthen

S1 Give two pieces of evidence of each of the following factors in the Revolt of the Northern Earls in 1569.

   a Political factors   **b** Religious factors

S2 Give one important outcome for the each of the plots against Elizabeth I: the Revolt of the Northern Earls; the Ridolfi, Throckmorton and Babington plots.

S3 Give three reasons why Sir Francis Walsingham's spy network was so effective.

Challenge

C1 Give three reasons why the Revolt of the Northern Earls in 1569 was such a major threat to Elizabeth I.

C2 Compare the threats to Elizabeth I from 1571–86. Which was the most serious and why?

C3 Explain why Mary, Queen of Scots, was executed in 1587 and not earlier.

If you are not confident about any of these questions, your teacher can give you some hints.

2.2 Relations with Spain

Learning objectives

- Understand Elizabeth I's foreign policy aims, and how that affected relations with Spain.

Timeline

The decline in Anglo–Spanish relations, 1570–84

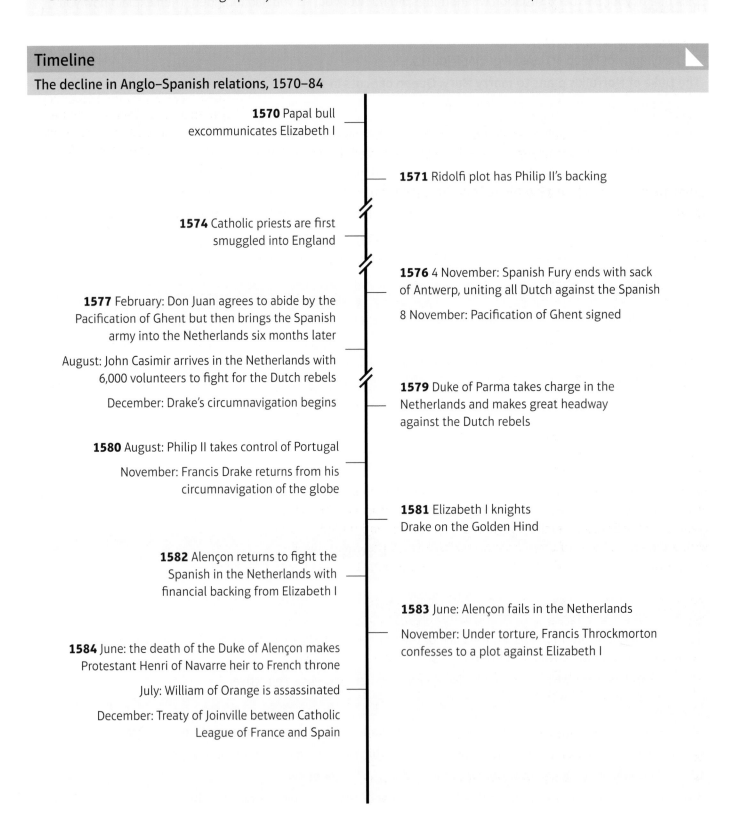

1570 Papal bull excommunicates Elizabeth I

1571 Ridolfi plot has Philip II's backing

1574 Catholic priests are first smuggled into England

1576 4 November: Spanish Fury ends with sack of Antwerp, uniting all Dutch against the Spanish

8 November: Pacification of Ghent signed

1577 February: Don Juan agrees to abide by the Pacification of Ghent but then brings the Spanish army into the Netherlands six months later

August: John Casimir arrives in the Netherlands with 6,000 volunteers to fight for the Dutch rebels

December: Drake's circumnavigation begins

1579 Duke of Parma takes charge in the Netherlands and makes great headway against the Dutch rebels

1580 August: Philip II takes control of Portugal

November: Francis Drake returns from his circumnavigation of the globe

1581 Elizabeth I knights Drake on the Golden Hind

1582 Alençon returns to fight the Spanish in the Netherlands with financial backing from Elizabeth I

1583 June: Alençon fails in the Netherlands

November: Under torture, Francis Throckmorton confesses to a plot against Elizabeth I

1584 June: the death of the Duke of Alençon makes Protestant Henri of Navarre heir to French throne

July: William of Orange is assassinated

December: Treaty of Joinville between Catholic League of France and Spain

Elizabeth I's foreign policy aims

For Elizabeth I, the pressures of ruling England influenced much of her foreign policy*. These pressures came from a lack of resources (England was far less wealthy and had a much smaller population than Spain or France) and England's religious divisions.

Elizabeth's foreign policy aims can be summarised as:

- developing and improving trade to benefit the English economy
- protecting England's borders
- protecting the English throne
- avoiding war, which would cost a lot of money and could potentially lead to Elizabeth being overthrown, if English rebels supported the enemy.

Commercial rivalry: the New World*, privateers* and Drake

During Elizabeth I's reign, English merchants began to explore new markets and trading partners. They went to Hamburg, Russia, China, India, Persia and Turkey. There were also huge profits to be made in the New World. However, English merchants faced problems in developing trade.

- Spain controlled the Netherlands, England's main route into European markets. Antwerp was particularly important to English trade in the Netherlands.
- Spain controlled much of the New World where there were valuable, new trading opportunities.

Spain claimed much of the Americas as its own, including Florida, the Caribbean, Mexico, Panama, Chile and Peru. The profits to be made in the New World were potentially enormous. There were valuable crops such as tobacco and sugar cane and huge supplies of silver. However, anyone who wanted to trade there needed a licence from Spain, which were very hard to come by. Many English merchants ignored Spain's rules and traded illegally, without licences. Some of them even attacked Spanish ports and shipping. Philip II could not ignore this challenge to Spain's interests in the New World.

Key terms
Foreign policy* The aims and objectives that guide a nation's relations with other states. The general aim is to benefit the nation. Objectives can include: trade, expanding into more territory and / or gaining more economic resources and building alliances. Foreign policy can focus on defending what a country has (a defensive policy) or conquering other lands (an aggressive policy).
New World* North and South America. Europeans were only aware of their existence from 1492.
Privateer* Historically, individuals (usually merchants or explorers) with their own armed ships that capture other ships for their cargoes, often with the authorisation or support of their government.

Activities ?

Francis Drake features strongly in the following sections of this book. As you find out more about him, consider Interpretation 1. You could do some more research on Drake and New World trade, too. For example, at this time, Europeans, including Drake, began exploiting the African slave trade.

1 List evidence for and against Drake as an English hero.

2 Why would the Elizabethans have seen Drake as a hero?

3 Why do some modern historians not see Drake as a hero?

Interpretation 1

Historian Angus Konstam talks about Francis Drake in *The Great Expedition* (2011).

… in 1586 England had a national hero who seemed capable of achieving anything he wanted. The boost to national morale was incalculable. As the prospects of war loomed ever larger, at least England could count on men like Sir Francis Drake to protect them from the wrath of the Spanish. The irony … is that if anyone helped bring about this war, it was Drake himself.

Francis Drake

Francis Drake was an English merchant who made his name and fortune trading in the New World. He also made huge sums of money for people who invested in his voyages, including Elizabeth I. However, much of what he did could be considered as piracy. During an expedition to the West Indies in 1570–71, for example, he captured numerous Spanish ships, and seized their cargoes.

In 1572, Elizabeth I hired Drake as a privateer. She got a good return on the money she invested in his voyage. Drake went to Panama, where he captured £40,000 of Spanish silver. However, Elizabeth's decision to back him was risky as it could have provoked further conflict with Spain. This was only avoided because by 1573, when Drake returned to England, both Philip II and Elizabeth were trying to improve Anglo–Spanish relations. Philip's anger at what he saw as English piracy meant that Elizabeth did not publicly welcome Drake home. Privately, however, she was impressed with his achievements.

In November 1577, Drake again set off for the New World. Elizabeth I's official plan was for him to sail around the tip of South America to its Pacific coastline. He was to bring gold, silver, spices and any other valuables back to England.

However, Elizabeth I also issued Drake with secret orders to attack Spain's colonies in the New World. By 1577, Anglo–Spanish relations were again getting worse and there were more fears of a Spanish invasion. Elizabeth, therefore, wanted to enrich England and disrupt Spain's valuable trade with its colonies (see Source A). It could also send a message of defiance to Philip II: Elizabeth I would not allow England to be dominated by Spain.

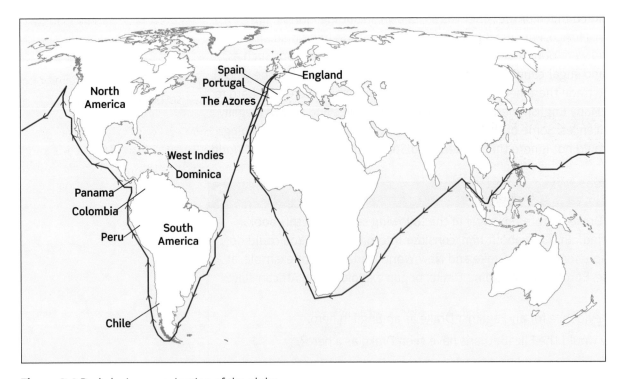

Figure 2.4 Drake's circumnavigation of the globe.

Drake's 1577–80 voyage became very famous because his actual route home led him to circumnavigate* the globe. He was the first Englishman to do so (and only the second person in history at that time). This was a major achievement as long sea voyages were exceptionally dangerous. Drake survived against the odds. He set off with five ships and only had one left, the **Golden Hind**, by the time he reached the Pacific Ocean.

Key term

Circumnavigate*
To travel all the way around the world.

Source A

From an account of Elizabeth I's meeting with Francis Drake before he set sail in 1577.

I would gladly be avenged on the King of Spain for diverse injuries that I have received.

Activities ?

1 Create a timeline of events for Drake, 1570-80.

2 Examine the significance of Drake's actions. Discuss with a partner which you think is the most significant for Elizabeth's relations with Spain.

3 Write a short paragraph explaining your answer.

The outcome of Drake's voyage

Once in the Pacific, Drake successfully plundered Spanish ports and ships along the coastline of Chile and Peru. He also claimed a region of north California in Elizabeth's name, calling it **New Albion**. It is estimated that when Drake returned to England in 1580, he brought £400,000 of Spanish treasure with

him. Although some of this went to the investors who had funded the voyage, it brought a great sum to the English Crown. Elizabeth was so impressed by his achievements that she knighted Drake on the deck of the Golden Hind. Philip II was outraged by this public display: to him Sir Francis Drake was nothing more than a pirate.

The significance of Drake's actions

- Drake's actions against Spain and her colonies, along with his claim to land in north California, made it clear that England did not accept Spain's domination of the Americas.

- Only one other sailor had successfully circumnavigated the globe, so Drake's success gave England a national hero and said something about England's strength as a seafaring nation.

- Drake boosted the Crown's finances at a time of growing concern over Spain's threat to England.

- Elizabeth's public knighting of Drake also sent a strong message of defiance to Spain.

Political and religious rivalry

In the 1500s, the nations of Europe were rivals. They competed for more territory. More territory meant more people, wealth and power. This rivalry often resulted in foreign policy that led to war. Religion was another source of conflict. Catholics saw Protestantism as something dangerous that had to be stamped out. Protestants saw Catholicism as an evil that wanted to destroy the 'true religion'. Philip II of Spain opposed Elizabeth's religious settlement in 1559.

Alliances were also part of foreign policy. They would be made according to what suited each country at the time. They would also be broken when they were no longer helpful. Spain and England had traditionally been allies. Once England became Protestant, however, that began to change.

In the 1500s, England was not as wealthy or powerful as Spain and France. Luckily, Spain and France competed to be the greatest European power and this rivalry was helpful to Elizabeth I. It meant that Spain and France each valued England as an ally against the other.

- France wanted to be allied to England because France was surrounded by Spanish territory except to the north (see Figure 1.8).
- Spain wanted to be allied to England because Elizabeth's fleet could help protect its ships sailing in the Channel to the Netherlands. Spain had controlled the Netherlands since the 15th century.

From 1567, however, Spanish ships were sailing to the Netherlands with troops and resources for the Duke of Alba's army. Its brutal campaign to stamp out Protestantism in the Netherlands caused great alarm to English Protestants. Elizabeth's leading Privy Councillors were Protestant, and they put pressure on her to help the Dutch Protestant rebels.

What did Elizabeth I do about the Netherlands?
Elizabeth I was reluctant to help Dutch Protestant rebels in the Netherlands. She wanted to avoid anything that could lead to war with Spain (see Figure 2.5).

Instead, she hoped to apply pressure on the Spanish to encourage them to agree to return the Netherlands to how they had been governed under an agreement made in 1548. This had given the Dutch a great deal of autonomy*, which Philip II had challenged, sparking the initial revolt in 1566.

Key term

Autonomy*

The right to self-government, so people of one country can manage its own affairs.

Elizabeth I applied pressure on Philip II in several ways.

- By indirectly (and unofficially) helping Dutch Protestants resist the Spanish
- By allowing Spanish shipping and colonies to come under attack from English privateers
- By pursuing friendly relations with France
- By encouraging others to fight the Spanish in the Netherlands.

In the 1570s, Elizabeth offered the promise of a marriage alliance with the heir to the French throne, the Duke of Alençon. She hoped to alarm Philip II of Spain enough to give the Dutch their independence back. When it didn't, she used her influence with the Duke of Alençon to encourage him to fight the Spanish in the Netherlands. This was a risky strategy, however, because Elizabeth did not want the French to be too successful in case they took control of the Netherlands themselves.

Figure 2.5 Reasons why Elizabeth I was reluctant to help Dutch Protestant rebels.

The Spanish Fury and the Pacification of Ghent, 1576

By 1576, the Spanish government in the Netherlands was all but bankrupt. Despite the silver and riches being brought in from the New World, the cost of war was too great for Spain to continue at the same pace.

Spain's forces in the Netherlands finally mutinied after months without pay, rampaging through Dutch provinces and finally sacking* Antwerp in November 1576. This was known as the Spanish Fury. The violence in Antwerp united all 17 Dutch provinces, Protestant and Catholic, together against Spain. They drew up the **Pacification of Ghent**, which demanded:

- all Spanish troops were to be expelled from the Netherlands
- the restoration of political autonomy
- an end to religious persecution.

Elizabeth sent a loan of £100,000 to the Dutch rebels and agreed (at some point in the future) to send an expeditionary force* to the Netherlands to help ensure that the Pacification of Ghent was carried out. In February 1577, Philip II's brother, Don Juan, arrived in the Netherlands and agreed to all the terms of the 17 united provinces. It must have seemed to Elizabeth that she had achieved her goals.

> ### Key terms
>
> **Sacking***
> To rob a town or city using violence, causing a lot of damage, usually in wartime.
>
> **Expeditionary force***
> An armed force sent to a foreign country to achieve a specific function or objective.

Source B

Engraving showing mutinying Spanish troops sacking Antwerp in 1576. It was made by the Dutch artist Franz Hogenberg in 1576.

8 Als nun die Spaniard die vberhandt   Das karmen in dieser großer not   Seint jung vnd alt beid man vnd weib   Vnd so da durch hinaus gewaden   Anno Dñj.

A missed opportunity?

Despite Elizabeth's optimism, less than six months after agreeing terms, Philip II sent a new army to attack the Dutch. This dashed any hopes that Elizabeth I had achieved her aims in the Netherlands. She hired a mercenary*, John Casimir, and financed him to raise an army of 6,000 English and Scottish volunteers to help the Dutch. The fact that it was volunteers led by a mercenary was important. It meant that Elizabeth was not officially sending an English army to fight the Spanish in her name. Spain and England were therefore not officially at war. The plan, however, backfired. Casimir's forces devastated Dutch Catholic churches, helping to persuade Dutch Catholics to make peace with Spain.

Privy Councillors, like the Earl of Leicester, urged Elizabeth to intervene in the Netherlands directly. In 1578, the situation there was potentially promising enough for a complete Dutch victory. An independent Netherlands would be a strong, Protestant ally for England against Spain. Elizabeth, however, hesitated. Disappointed at her lack of commitment to their cause, the Dutch asked France for help. The Duke of Alençon agreed and came with an army to fight the Spanish.

By 1579, the situation in the Netherlands had changed. The Duke of Parma, who had been sent to the Netherlands by Philip II, was a far more effective military leader than Don Juan and the Spanish soon had the upper hand.

Key term

Mercenary*

A soldier who fights for money rather than a nation or cause.

The international situation in 1578	The international situation in 1579
• Spain was financially weak.	• Spain was still financially weak.
• France and England were allies.	• France and England were still allies.
• Don Juan's army was not very successful.	• Don Juan was replaced by the Duke of Parma as governor of the Netherlands.
• The Dutch leader, William of Orange, was popular and able to rally all the Dutch states against the Spanish, uniting Catholics and Protestants.	• Spain's armies began making headway against the Dutch.
• The Duke of Alençon led an army into the Netherlands to fight the Spanish.	• John Casimir's troops violently attacked Catholic churches in the Netherlands.
	• The southern Dutch Catholic provinces made peace with the Spanish.
	• Alençon withdrew from the Netherlands.

Activity ?

Work in pairs. One of you must decide how far Spain's improving position in the Netherlands in 1579 was a result of Elizabeth I's mistakes. The other must decide how far it was down to factors beyond her control. Compare findings. Make a joint decision about how far Elizabeth I was to blame. Use a value continuum like the one below to illustrate your answer.

100% Elizabeth's
mistakes

100% beyond
her control

Spain's fortunes restored, 1580–84

The Duke of Alençon came to England in October 1581. Elizabeth agreed to give him £70,000 for support in the Netherlands (with the promise of more later). In 1580, Philip II gained Portugal, along with its empire and naval forces. Spain's new strength and wealth alarmed Elizabeth. Perhaps this is why she still refused to intervene in the Netherlands: the odds against England were now even greater. Instead, Elizabeth once more turned to France. Alençon returned to the Netherlands in 1582, but again failed. He returned to France in 1583.

Interpretation 2 sees Elizabeth herself as the key reason for her foreign policy's failure.

Interpretation 2

An extract about Elizabeth's involvement in the Netherlands from *Elizabeth I: Meeting the Challenge, England 1541–1603* (2008) by John Warren.

> … nothing Elizabeth had done had contributed towards a successful resolution [in the Netherlands] in line with English interests. Instead, she had managed to alienate Spain without earning the trust of the Netherlands. The unhappy prospect of a complete Spanish victory loomed.

1584: a turning point in Anglo–Spanish relations

Circumstances beyond Elizabeth's control made England's situation even more hazardous by the end of 1584: on 10 June, the Duke of Alençon died. Only one month later, on 10 July, William of Orange, the leader of the Dutch Protestant rebels, was assassinated.

Should England help the Dutch? Despite the change in circumstances, Elizabeth I still preferred a cautious approach. Cecil agreed. Others, led by the Earl of Leicester, urged Elizabeth to intervene in the Netherlands. The Privy Council debated the issue long and hard from autumn 1584 until summer 1585. As it turned out, the decision was all but made for them.

At the end of 1584, the French Catholic League signed the **Treaty of Joinville** with Philip II to secure his help against French Protestants. In 1585, the King of France signed up to the Catholic League's aim of ridding France of heresy. Effectively this meant that Catholic France and Spain were now allies against Protestantism.

Duke of Alençon
Died 10 June 1584

William of Orange
Assassinated 10 July 1584

The deaths of the Duke of Alençon and William of Orange cause problems for Elizabeth's foreign policy because:

- he could no longer fight the Spanish in the Netherlands
- although France's new heir to the throne was Henri of Navarre, a Protestant, leading French Catholics formed a Catholic League to stop him
- it led to a religious war in France, meaning it was too unstable to be a useful ally to England.

- it showed how easy it was for a leader like Elizabeth to be assassinated
- Dutch Protestants needed a leader and looked to Elizabeth. She did not want this role as she could be seen as trying to overthrow Philip II.
- without a leader, the Dutch rebels could be defeated by Spain, leaving England as Philip II's next target.

Figure 2.6 The impact of the deaths of the Duke of Alençon and William of Orange on Elizabeth I's foreign policy.

Activities ?

1 Explain the importance of the following events.

   a The Spanish Fury and Pacification of Ghent.

   b Spain's position strengthened after taking control of Portugal.

   c The deaths of Alençon and William of Orange.

2 Why was there so much uncertainty between 1584–5 over whether to help the Dutch? Explain the different points-of-view with reference to the events and changing circumstances from 1580. You could write this as a script or dialogue with Lord Burghley and the Earl of Leicester trying to persuade Elizabeth I of their case. It is important for you to show you can understand the situation England was in and the different points-of-view about what to do.

Exam-style question, Section B

'The decline in Anglo–Spanish relations in the years 1569–85 was caused by Elizabeth I'. How far do you agree?

You may use the following in your answer:

- Drake's voyages to the New World
- The Netherlands.

You **must** also use information of your own.

16 marks

Exam tip

Planning your answers is a very important part of exam success.

This question tests your ability not only to explain why something happened but also to analyse Elizabeth I's role. It is important to deal with **at least** three factors in total. You may use the information provided by the question, but to gain a top mark, you must provide information of your own. To do this, you **must** take time to plan.

Summary

- Relations with Spain worsened between 1569 and 1585.
- Elizabeth I's foreign policy was defensive – she wanted to avoid war.
- The Dutch Revolt led to a large Spanish military force being sent to the Netherlands. It was seen as very threatening to England.
- English support for Dutch rebels was limited and indirect until 1585.
- Elizabeth I used friendship with France as well as mercenaries to support the Dutch rebels.
- Sir Francis Drake provoked Philip II's anger with his actions in the New World.
- Members of Elizabeth I's Privy Council were frustrated by her hesitation, especially in 1578.
- In 1584, circumstances beyond Elizabeth I's control finally led to her intervening directly in the Netherlands in 1585.

Checkpoint

Strengthen

S1 Give two aims of Elizabeth I's foreign policy.

S2 Write a sentence explaining the importance of the following events in worsening Anglo–Spanish relations 1569–84.

    a Francis Drake's expeditions to the New World.

    b The Dutch Revolt in the Netherlands (including the Pacification of Ghent in 1576).

    c The Treaty of Joinville in 1584.

S3 Elizabeth I tried to avoid direct conflict with Spain but still indirectly put pressure on Spain to leave the Netherlands alone. Describe, and give examples, of two ways in which she did this.

Challenge

C1 Identify one turning point in the deterioration of Anglo–Spanish relations in the 1570s and explain its importance.

C2 Write a paragraph, with examples from the 1570s and 1580s, explaining how Elizabeth I caused the deterioration in Anglo–Spanish relations?

C3 Write a paragraph, with examples from the 1570s and 1580s, explaining how Philip II caused the deterioration in Anglo–Spanish relations?

C4 Why was the death of the Duke of Alençon in 1584 so important for Elizabeth I?

C5 Explain why Elizabeth I knighted Francis Drake in 1581. You must refer to both what he had achieved, and the circumstances the queen faced, by 1581.

To help with these questions, you might find it useful to draw a timeline dating the important moments in Anglo–Spanish relations in the 1570s and 1580s.

2.3 Outbreak of war with Spain, 1585–88

Learning objectives

- Understand how England's involvement in the Netherlands encouraged war with Spain.

England's direct involvement in the Netherlands 1585–88

How and why did Elizabeth I change her foreign policy?

After the Treaty of Joinville was signed in 1584, Elizabeth could no longer avoid direct intervention in the Netherlands.

Elizabeth takes direct action, 1585

In June 1585, Dutch Protestant representatives came to England offering Elizabeth I the sovereignty of the Netherlands. She refused, as it would mean deposing King Philip II, something she was still unwilling to do: Elizabeth refused to depose an anointed monarch. Instead, on 10 August 1585, Elizabeth I signed the **Treaty of Nonsuch** with the Dutch Protestants. It effectively put England and Spain at war: Elizabeth had agreed to intervene directly in the Netherlands on the side of the rebels. Philip II thought the English should stay out of the Netherlands as they belonged to Spain. England would finance an army of 7,400 English troops under a commander of her choosing, who would work with the rebels' government, the Council of State. The man she chose was her long-time favourite, Robert Dudley, Earl of Leicester.

In October 1585, Elizabeth also sent Sir Francis Drake to raid Spanish New World settlements, with the aim of disrupting Philip II's flow of resource and finances. However, rather than deterring Philip, Drake only succeeded in angering him. Philip told the pope he intended to invade England at the end of 1585.

Extend your knowledge

The Treaty of Berwick

In 1586, England and Scotland signed the Treaty of Berwick. This made England's northern borders much more secure, enabling Elizabeth to focus on the Netherlands. The terms of the treaty were:

- Elizabeth I and James VI agreed to maintain Protestantism as their countries' religion
- Elizabeth I and James VI agreed to help each other if invaded.

Robert Dudley in the Netherlands, 1585–87

Source A

A picture of Robert Dudley, Earl of Leicester, painted in 1585.

England's intervention in the Netherlands was not a great success. Elizabeth did not want to take the initiative: she was still hoping to negotiate with Spain. Leicester was therefore not given enough money for men or supplies to mount a large campaign.

The campaign started badly. In January 1586, Leicester accepted the title of **Governor General of the Netherlands** on Elizabeth's behalf. Elizabeth was furious: this implied she was deposing Philip II as king of the Netherlands.

In the summer of 1586, English forces only managed to slow the Duke of Parma's advance through the Netherlands. In September, they did take some forts outside the Spanish controlled town of Zutphen. In January 1587, however, they lost one, Zutphen Fort, when it was handed over by an English captain, Rowland York. He defected to the Spanish along with Sir William Stanley. Stanley had been the governor of the town Deventer and gave it to the Spanish. After this, the Dutch found it hard to trust Leicester, especially because he had appointed Stanley.

Leicester was called back to England in November 1586 but returned to the Netherlands in June 1587. He still didn't have enough men or supplies. However, he managed to cause the Duke of Parma enough problems to prevent him from taking the major, deep-water port of Ostend. Parma's failure to capture any deep-water ports proved important in the failure of the Armada in 1588 (see page 62). Elizabeth recalled Leicester from the Netherlands for good at the end of 1587.

The English campaign in the Netherlands was not successful between 1586 and 1588 for three main reasons.

1 Elizabeth was never fully behind the rebels. She still hoped to negotiate with Spain and did not give Leicester the funds necessary to mount a large campaign.

2 Leicester and Elizabeth had different aims in the Netherlands. Leicester wanted to liberate the Netherlands from the Spanish, making it independent. Elizabeth wanted a return to how the Netherlands had been governed in 1548.

3 Relations between the English and Dutch leaders were poor because of Elizabeth's lack of commitment.

Drake sings the King of Spain's beard, 1587

Since January 1586, Spain had been preparing the Armada, Philip II's mighty invasion fleet. In March 1587, Elizabeth ordered Francis Drake to attack Spain's navy. On 19 April, he sailed into Cadiz harbour, Spain's most important Atlantic port, and over three days destroyed 30 ships as well as a great deal of the fleet's provisions. The attack on Cadiz is known as the '**singeing of the King of Spain's beard**'.

Drake then spent several weeks attacking the coast of Portugal before heading to the Azores. His aim was to capture Spanish treasure ships bringing silver from Spain's New World colonies. Although he only captured one, Spain had to break off from building the Armada to defend itself against Drake. The disruption Drake caused did not stop the Armada but it was delayed by a year. This bought England more time to prepare.

Activity   ?

Draw a table with three columns. The column headings are: 'Politics', 'Religion' and 'Role of the Individual'. In each column list as much evidence as you can to show how each of the three factors led to the decline in Anglo–Spanish relations 1585–88.

Summary

- Elizabeth I promised to help the Dutch and signed the Treaty of Nonsuch in 1585.
- However, England's intervention in the Netherlands was not very successful.
- The Earl of Leicester made little progress in the Netherlands as he did not have enough men or resources and so did not get on well with the Dutch.
- Elizabeth sent Sir Francis Drake to raid Spanish New World settlements in 1585.
- In 1587, Drake 'singed the King of Spain's beard' and delayed the launch of the Armada.

Checkpoint

Strengthen

S1 Give one term from the Treaty of Nonsuch and one reason Elizabeth I agreed to the treaty.

S2 Give two reasons why the Earl of Leicester failed in the Netherlands.

S3 Give two examples when Francis Drake angered Philip II and two examples in which he helped England after 1585.

Challenge

C1 Explain how a combination of two factors led to the outbreak of war between England and Spain. Factors could include religion, the Dutch Revolt, politics, or the role of the individual, such as Elizabeth I, Philip II, or Francis Drake.

C2 Explain why Elizabeth was partly to blame for the Earl of Leicester's failure in the Netherlands.

These questions ask you to take into consideration not just things in this section, but everything you have learned in Chapter 2 so far. If you are struggling, review your notes from the previous sections of this chapter.

2.4 The Armada

Why did Philip II launch the Spanish Armada?

Mary, Queen of Scots' execution in 1587 is often mistakenly thought to be the cause of the launch of the Spanish Armada. The actual decision, however, had been taken as early as October 1585.

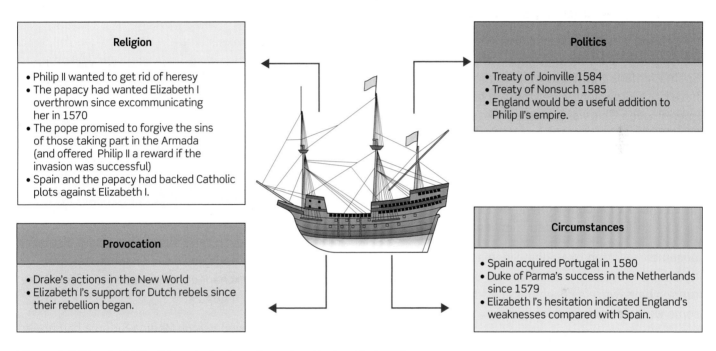

Religion

- Philip II wanted to get rid of heresy
- The papacy had wanted Elizabeth I overthrown since excommunicating her in 1570
- The pope promised to forgive the sins of those taking part in the Armada (and offered Philip II a reward if the invasion was successful)
- Spain and the papacy had backed Catholic plots against Elizabeth I.

Politics

- Treaty of Joinville 1584
- Treaty of Nonsuch 1585
- England would be a useful addition to Philip II's empire.

Provocation

- Drake's actions in the New World
- Elizabeth I's support for Dutch rebels since their rebellion began.

Circumstances

- Spain acquired Portugal in 1580
- Duke of Parma's success in the Netherlands since 1579
- Elizabeth I's hesitation indicated England's weaknesses compared with Spain.

Figure 2.7 Why did Philip II launch the Armada against England in 1588?

Philip's strategy

With 130 ships, 2,431 guns and around 30,000 men, Philip II's Armada was the largest fleet Europe had ever seen. Under the command of the Duke of Medina-Sidonia, it was ordered to sail along the English Channel to the Netherlands. There it would join up with the Duke of Parma. Together they would transport 27,000 troops to Kent and then Parma would march on London, depose Elizabeth and impose a new, Catholic government in England.

How did England defeat the Spanish Armada?

English ship design

One reason for English victory was its **ships**. Another was **long term planning**. The treasurer of the navy, John Hawkins, had advised Elizabeth years before that English warships needed to be fast and easily manoeuvrable so they could turn their guns on the enemy quicker.

New ships, known as **galleons**, were built from the early 1570s. They were designed to be easier and faster to manoeuvre.

In English ships, the cannons were mounted on smaller gun carriages than on Spanish ships. When a cannon is fired it recoils quite a long way. The decks on English ships had enough space for cannon to recoil, be quickly reloaded by a small team of men and then pushed back through the gun port. This meant that English ships could fire more cannon balls at the Spanish with more speed.

However, although galleons were some of the best warships in the world, by 1588 England had only 24 of these new ships. Therefore, galleons alone cannot explain Spain's defeat.

Spanish supplies

Spain's Armada was not as well supplied as it might have been. Provisions were stored in barrels made of inferior wood. This was because Drake's raid on Cadiz had destroyed so many barrels that new ones had to be made quickly. Delays in setting sail and bad weather meant that by the time the English engaged the Armada, it had already been at sea for over ten weeks. When the English boarded the first Spanish ship they captured, they found its food supplies already rotting.

Documents written by Medina-Sidonia also indicate that the Armada was low on supplies of the necessary cannon balls, while archaeological evidence suggests some were also of very poor quality.

Planning and communications issues

Philip II's plan required Medina-Sidonia to join with Parma, who was to command a fleet from the Netherlands. This was a weakness for two reasons.

1   The Duke of Parma did not control any deep-sea ports (which large war ships needed) in the Netherlands. Instead he had to use lots of small ships. This meant it would take 48 hours to load, man and set sail once word came from the Duke of Medina-Sidonia to join his fleet.

2   Communications between Medina-Sidonia and Parma had to go by sea and were therefore unreliable. It took a week for word to reach Parma that Medina-Sidonia was in the Channel. By this time, Medina-Sidonia was off Calais waiting to engage the English. Although his message got through to Parma eventually, it was too late.

His fleet would not be ready to set sail for another 48 hours and the English were ready to attack.

English tactics

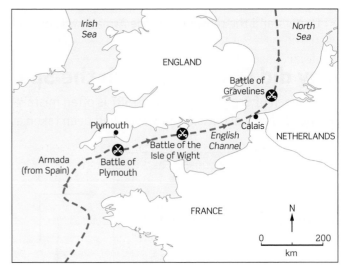

Figure 2.8 The course of the Armada.

The Armada was spotted in the English Channel on 29 July 1588. The English, having set sail from Plymouth, opened fire on 31 July and captured two ships. The English fleet, however, generally kept at a safe distance and chased the Armada down the Channel. However, there were some exchanges of heavy cannon fire off the Isle of Wight on 3–4 August.

This exchange proved useful. Medina-Sidonia had hoped to anchor safely off the Isle of Wight. Stopping for a couple of days might have meant that Parma received Medina-Sidonia's messages in enough time to get the Dutch fleet ready for his arrival.

During the engagement off the Isle of Wight, the English were able to fire as many as six times more cannon balls than the Spanish and from further away. The Earl of Nottingham, a commander of the English fleet, realised the advantage this gave England and decided to conserve cannon balls for the decisive battle.

The Battle of Gravelines, 8 August 1588

On the night of 6 August, the English sent fireships* in amongst the Spanish fleet. Although they did very little actual damage to the Spanish ships, they created havoc by scattering the Armada. When it regrouped on 8 August, the English engaged the Spanish in the Battle of Gravelines.

Medina-Sidonia had to fight without Parma's ships, which were not ready. Up against faster, more mobile English ships with cannons that were easier to load, the Armada was defeated and scattered by the winds. In fact, most of the destruction was done by the gales that wrecked Spanish ships as they tried to return home through the treacherous waters off the Scottish and Irish coasts. Thousands were killed.

Key term

Fireships*

Empty ships set on fire and sent in the direction of the enemy to cause damage and confusion.

Should Philip II take the blame for defeat?

Although Philip II had consulted his military commanders before the Armada sailed, he seems to have ignored their suggestions, their criticisms and their concerns. On the other hand, Elizabeth I left the key decisions to her commanders: Francis Drake, the Earl of Nottingham and Lord Seymour. Interpretation 1 is very clear about Philip II's role in the defeat of the Armada.

Interpretation 1

One interpretation discussing why Philip II failed to invade England in 1588 from 'Why The Armada Failed' in *History Today Magazine* (1988).

Here, then, lay Philip's true error: he was not only an armchair strategist, but an armchair tactician too … the final version [of his plans] depended for success upon a tactical edge which Spain's ships simply did not possess. In this disharmony between strategy and tactics, therefore, lies the true explanation of the Armada's fate.

What were the consequences of the English victory over the Spanish Armada?

After the Battle of Gravelines, Elizabeth I addressed her troops at Tilbury, where they were still assembled ready to defend England from a possible invasion from the Netherlands by the Duke of Parma. Source A is an extract from this famous speech.

Source A

Excerpt from Elizabeth I's speech to her troops at Tilbury, August 1588.

Let tyrants fear … I am come amongst you, … being resolved, in the midst and heat of the battle, to live and die amongst you all; to lay down for my God, and for my kingdom, and my people, my honour and my blood, even in the dust.

I know I have the body but of a weak and feeble woman; but I have the heart and stomach of a king, and of a king of England too, and think foul scorn that Parma or Spain, or any prince of Europe, should dare to invade the borders of my realm.

Victory over the Armada gave Elizabeth I a great propaganda* victory. A new portrait was commissioned (see Source B), the queen was the centre of a great parade in London and a special commemorative medal was struck. It said 'God blew, and they were scattered'. This was an important point: God clearly seemed to favour Protestantism, and Elizabeth was eager to emphasise this.

Key term

Propaganda*

Biased information used to promote a point-of-view.

Source B

The Armada portrait of Elizabeth I, painted in 1588 by George Gower.

England itself had survived an attack by a more powerful foe. This helped nurture a feeling of English pride. It also encouraged the Dutch rebels to renew their fight against the Spanish. Had Philip II been successful, any English support for Dutch Protestants would have ended. As it was, the Anglo–Dutch alliance became stronger than ever before.

The defeat of the Armada also showed the strength of the English navy. After 1588, it also gave England the confidence to trade and explore more widely on the open sea.

Nevertheless, Philip II did not give up. The battle was won but the war continued for the remainder of Elizabeth's reign. The failure of the Armada might have been a setback, but his belief that Catholicism was the true religion was unshaken. However, the defeat cost Spain dearly, both financially and in terms of its power. The Armada marked the beginning of a long decline in Spanish fortunes.

Figure 2.9 Reasons for the defeat of the Armada in 1588.

Summary

- The Armada was the Spanish fleet sent to invade England in 1588.
- The English fleet set out from Plymouth and followed the Armada to Calais.
- The Armada had problems with supplies and communications.
- The English had faster ships that could fire more cannon balls from a greater distance.
- The Battle of Gravelines did substantial damage to the Armada.
- After Gravelines, the Armada headed north and thousands lost their lives in shipwrecks.
- The defeat of the Armada was a great propaganda boost for Elizabeth I, England and Protestantism in Europe.

Checkpoint

Strengthen

S1 Describe the key features of Philip II's plan to invade England.

S2 Give two advantages English ships had over Spanish ships.

S3 Give one example in which the Armada benefitted Elizabeth I.

Challenge

C1 Identify a key turning point in the events that lead to the defeat of the Spanish Armada and explain your choice.

C2 Explain the importance of each of the following in the defeat of the Armada.
- Philip II
- John Hawkins
- English cannon

C3 Explain the significance of the Spanish Armada on Anglo–Spanish relations.

If you are not confident about any of these questions, form a group with other students, discuss the answers and then record your conclusions. Your teacher can give you some hints.

Recap: Challenges to Elizabeth at home and abroad, 1569–88

1 What and when were the four key plots against Elizabeth I?

2 Give two reasons why the northern earls revolted in 1569.

3 Give one reason why the 1570 papal bull of excommunication was so significant.

4 Who was John Hart and what did he do?

5 Supply two items stated by the Act for the Preservation of the Queen's Safety, 1585.

6 Why was the New World so important to Spain?

7 Between which years did Sir Francis Drake circumnavigate the globe?

8 Give two examples when Elizabeth I indirectly supported the Dutch Rebellion.

9 When was the Battle of Gravelines?

10 Give two reasons why the Spanish Armada failed.

Activity

Make a timeline of the key events of the Armada from 31 July to 8 August 1588.

Activities

1 Work in groups of four. Study Figure 2.7 on page 61. Each take one factor explaining why Philip II used the Armada in 1588. Explain and provide evidence for your factor.

2 Once you have done your research, feedback to each other. Pick one factor. Now make as many links as you can to other factors. Do this with the other three factors.

3 Which factor includes the most links to other factors?

Activities

1 Work in pairs to make a bar chart showing how the level of threat faced by Elizabeth I changed from 1569–1588. You will need a horizontal axis on which you can mark all 20 years. The vertical axis will show the level of threat faced by Elizabeth I. Use a scale of 0–10. Decide how the threat to Elizabeth I developed year-on-year. A score of 10 would mean that England was invaded or Elizabeth I was overthrown. A score of 0 would mean no threat to Elizabeth I, at home or abroad.

You must remember that although there are some years when nothing important happens, it does not mean that there was no threat. In 1575, for example, the Spanish were still in the Netherlands and Catholic priests had started arriving in England. If you wish, you could research years for which you have no information.

2 Compare the events of 1569 and 1588. Would Elizabeth I have felt more under threat at the end of 1569 or 1588? Write a paragraph explaining your answer.

3 Write two paragraphs comparing the similarities and differences in the threats Elizabeth I faced in 1558–69 with those of 1570–88.

4 Why was Elizabeth I able to survive the challenges she faced during 1569–88? Write one paragraph on how she survived domestic challenges, and one on foreign challenges.

Writing historically: building sentences

Successful historical writing uses a range of sentence structures to achieve clarity, precision and emphasis.

Learning outcomes

By the end of this lesson, you will understand how to:

- use and position subordinate clauses to link ideas with clarity and precision
- manipulate sentence structure to emphasise key ideas.

Definitions

Clause: a group of words or unit of meaning that contains a verb and can form part or all of a sentence.

Single clause sentence: a sentence containing just one clause.

Subordinating conjunction: a word used to link a dependent clause to the main clause of a sentence.

Compare the two drafts of sentences below, written in response to this exam-style question:

> Explain why Philip II launched the Armada against England in 1588.
>
> **(12 marks)**

These points are written in pairs of unlinked, **single clause sentences**.	The relationship between these points is made clear with subordinating conjunctions.
Philip was angry with Elizabeth. She had offered support to Dutch Protestants who were rebelling against Spain.	Philip was angry with Elizabeth because she had offered support to Dutch Protestants who were rebelling against Spain.
Mary, Queen of Scots was executed in 1587. The Armada was already being prepared when news of the execution reached Philip.	Although Mary, Queen of Scots was executed in 1587, the Armada was already being prepared when news of the execution reached Philip.
Elizabeth was excommunicated by the pope in 1570. Philip openly supported all plots against Elizabeth's life.	After Elizabeth was excommunicated by the pope in 1570, Philip openly supported all plots against Elizabeth's life.

1. Which responses are more clearly expressed? Write a sentence or two explaining your answer.

Subordinating conjunctions can link ideas to indicate:

- an explanation: (e.g. 'because', 'as', 'in order that')
- a condition: (e.g. 'if', 'unless')
- a comparison: (e.g. although, whereas)
- a sequence: (e.g. 'when', 'as', 'before', 'until' etc.)

2. In how many different ways can you use subordinating conjunctions to link these pairs of ideas, clearly expressing the relationship between them?

- Mary, Queen of Scots, caused Elizabeth I a lot of trouble. Mary came to England as the Catholic alternative to Elizabeth's Protestant rule.

- Mary was involved in many plots against Elizabeth. She had the support of Philip II and the pope.

How can I structure my sentences for clarity and emphasis?

In sentences where ideas are linked with subordinate conjunctions, there is:

- a main clause that gives the central point of the sentence

- a dependent, subordinate clause that adds more information about that central point.

Different sentence structures can alter the emphasis of your writing. Look at these sentences that have been used to introduce responses to the exam-style question on the previous page:

Compare these two versions of the first sentence:

> *Although Mary, Queen of Scots was executed in 1587,* the Armada was already being prepared when news of the execution reached Philip. *The Armada sailed in 1588.*

This is the main clause in this sentence

This is a subordinate clause. It is linked to the main clause with a subordinating conjunction.

> The Armada was already being prepared when news of the execution reached Philip, *although Mary, Queen of Scots was executed in 1587. The Armada sailed in 1588.*

3a. Which clause is given more emphasis in each version? Why?

   b. Which version do you prefer? Write a sentence or two explaining your decision.

In both responses, the second sentence is much shorter than the first sentence.

4. Why do you think the writer chose to give this point additional emphasis by structuring it as a short sentence? Write a sentence or two explaining your ideas.

5a. Experiment with different ways of sequencing the three pieces of information in the student's response above, linking all, some, or none of them with subordinating conjunctions:

- Mary, Queen of Scots was executed in 1587
- the Armada was already being prepared
- the Armada sailed in 1588.

   b. Which version do you prefer? One of yours, or the original version? Write a sentence or two explaining your decision.

Improving an answer

6. Now look at the notes below written in response to the exam-style question on the previous page.

> *Philip was a staunch Catholic.*
>
> *Elizabeth had offered support to Dutch Protestants.*
>
> *Elizabeth was excommunicated by the pope in 1570.*
>
> *Throckmorton and Babington plots, supported by Philip and the pope.*
>
> *The Armada sailed in 1588.*

   a. Experiment with different ways of sequencing and structuring all the information in sentences. Try to write at least three different versions.

   b. Which version do you prefer? Write a sentence or two explaining your decision.

03 | Elizabethan society in the Age of Exploration, 1558–88

Elizabeth I's reign was a time of expansion, with growth in many different areas of society and daily life.

There were new territories to be conquered in the New World, where it was believed there were great fortunes to be made. This opened up more opportunities in commerce. There was also expansion in ideas and different ways of thinking, including poetry, drama, philosophy and science. This affected what was taught in schools and universities.

Plays, sports, games and other pastimes gave people a break from their worries and problems. For Elizabeth I, her courtiers and the nobility, these worries might mean concerns over England's religious problems or the threat of war with Spain. For business owners, merchants and skilled craftsmen, there were economic problems: trade could be badly affected by poor relations with Spain and conflict in the Netherlands. When there were conflicts, businesses failed and unemployment rose. For the landless or labouring poor, and those now unemployed, people faced poverty and even starvation.

Learning outcomes

By the end of this chapter, you will:

- know about the lives of ordinary Elizabethans, including how they spent their leisure time
- understand why the Elizabethans were so concerned about the poor, and how they tried to tackle the problem of poverty
- understand what made men like Francis Drake undertake long and difficult voyages to the Americas
- know and understand why the early English colonies that settled in North America struggled to survive.

Quando pilà et Sphæræ flectuntur corporis artus.

Corpus erit levius, pectus erit levius.

3.1 Education and leisure

- Understand Elizabethan attitudes to education.
- Know the different leisure activities pursued by Elizabethan society.

Education

Attitudes to education

Although there was no national system of schooling, education was becoming increasingly valuable in Elizabethan England. While attitudes to education were beginning to change, they still reflected the social hierarchy of the country. Education was not about nurturing talent and ambition, nor about allowing social mobility*. The existing social order was very important to Elizabethans and any education you might receive was aimed at preparing you for the life you were expected to lead. This meant it usually focused on practical skills, but could include basic literacy. Only a small percentage of children (and then, mainly boys) went to school at all. Very few girls received any formal education in Elizabethan England.

> **Key term**
>
> **Social mobility***
> Being able to change your position in society.

New influences on education

Some thinkers and writers in the 16th century, known as **humanists**, believed that learning was important in its own right. They didn't believe people should just be educated for practical reasons. They studied the work of ancient philosophers and mathematicians to develop a better understanding of the world. To them, education was important if people were to stop being so superstitious and fulfil their potential as human beings.

Protestants believed that people should be able to read the Bible in their own language, to develop their own relationship with God. This encouraged more people to become literate. Also, as business and trade developed, a basic education became more important to more people, especially in towns.

Nevertheless, it is important not to exaggerate the extent to which education developed in Elizabethan England. For most people, education was limited according to their place in the social hierarchy, and in rural areas, where farming remained a way of life, little had changed.

Education in the home

Nobility

The children of the nobility learned a variety of subjects such as foreign languages, including Latin and Greek, History, Philosophy, Government and Theology. As Elizabeth I was highly educated in these subjects, many noble families ensured that their daughters were, too. They also learned a variety of skills expected of upper class women, such as music, dancing, needlework, horse riding and archery. They were tutored at home, as were their brothers, but separately by the age of around seven. Boys were taught to be skilled in horse riding and archery too, and also fencing, swimming, wrestling and other sports thought fitting only for men.

The children of noble families were often sent to another noble household to finish their education. The eldest sons would inherit their fathers' titles, and so would have to learn how to become future noble men. Girls who went to another noble family would make useful social contacts, as well as perfect those skills expected of them as a noble woman.

Middling sorts and grammar schools

The greatest change in education in Elizabethan England was the development of grammar schools: 42 were founded in the 1560s, and 30 more in the 1570s. As a result, there were more schools in Elizabethan England than there had ever been before. Previously, the Church provided most of the minimal education available to children.

Source A

A 16th-century woodcut showing a teacher and his pupils.

Grammar schools were private schools set up for boys considered bright, who largely came from well-off families in towns – the sons of middling sorts: the gentry, professionals or wealthy business owners. Girls could not attend grammar schools. They were usually educated at home by their mothers, preparing them for married life and running a household.

Fees for grammar schools varied, and were often based upon how much property the boy's family owned. Some lower class boys who showed promise could also attend, and they did not have to pay fees. Their places were funded by people who left money to the schools in their will to provide education for those who would not be able to afford to go without help.

The school year was long, with holidays only at Christmas and Easter. School days were also long, beginning at 6 a.m. or 7 a.m., and lasting for almost ten hours. The focus of the curriculum was Latin (the best schools also taught Greek and French as well). The boys also studied ancient, classical historians and philosophers and writers such as Plato, Aristotle, Virgil and Seneca. There would also be time allocated for archery, chess, wrestling and running.

Below is a grammar school timetable. The timetable is based upon a document written for a grammar school in Wales. It is typical of grammar schools established throughout the 16th century and beyond. There was a great emphasis on memorising huge quantities of texts, especially Bible passages, many of which focused on teaching morals and manners. Debating was also important. Two or three boys would be expected to debate a topic set by the teacher. Public speaking and debating was thought essential for a well-educated Elizabethan gentleman.

As well as school Monday through to Friday (as shown in the timetable below), there was also school on a Saturday morning. There would often be more recitation of the week's lessons but also other activities.

	Monday–Thursday	Friday
6.00	Church – prayers	Church – prayers
7.00	Recite previous day's lessons by heart	Translate what was read the day before
7.30	Breakfast	Breakfast
8.00	Translation: Latin into English	Recite what has been learned so far this week
9.00	Study of works of classical scholars – History, Philosophy, Literature, Poetry	Recite what has been learned so far this week
11.00	Dinner	Dinner
12.00	Teacher questions class on what was read before dinner; homework marked while boys studied Latin or Greek grammar	Recite what has been learned so far this week
1.00	Translation to / from English, Latin, Greek or rehearse and act out classical plays	Recite what has been learned so far this week
3.30	Afternoon break	Recite what has been learned so far this week
4.00	Grammar – or recite what has been learned so far this week	Teacher reads classical texts to the class
5.00	School ends	School ends

Discipline and punishments

The teacher maintained discipline in the classroom. Outside the classroom, two boys were made monitors and had to report misbehaviour inside and outside school grounds, including in the street. Any boys reported were questioned on Mondays at 9 a.m. and punished, unless their behaviour was more serious, in which case, punishment was immediate.

Figure 3.1 Punishments in Elizabethan grammar schools.

Merchants and Craftsmen

Some grammar schools ran an alternative curriculum for the sons of merchants and craftsmen. These focused on more practical academic subjects, such as English, Writing, Arithmetic and Geography. This shows education reflecting what the economy needed, but still focused on preparing boys for the life they were expected to lead.

Skilled craftsmen and yeomen

There were grammar schools available for the children of craftsmen and yeomen farmers, although much of their education would come in the form of apprenticeships, where they would learn what was necessary to run the family business or farm.

For boys, whether children could go to school or not often depended on whether their family could manage without having them help in the family business or in the home. As school was not compulsory, a child's education depended on whether their parents valued a school-based education. Even then, some children would have to leave school at an early age to go to work or to become an apprentice* to a master craftsman.

Key term

Apprentice*

Someone learning a trade or a skill. In Elizabethan times, apprentices were not paid. In fact, it cost money to be an apprentice. Once qualified, skilled craftsmen usually enjoyed a very good standard of living.

Petty schools

Petty schools were often set up and run in a teacher's home. Boys whose parents could afford to send them to school began their education here, or, in the case of girls, in **Dame schools** (see below). They would learn Reading and Writing in English, as well as basic Arithmetic. Punishment was often harsh. Beating for poor behaviour or not doing well in lessons was common.

After attending the petty school, bright or well-off boys would go to a grammar school. According to the Elizabethan author William Harrison, by 1577, every town in England had a grammar school.

Schools for girls

Girls of all classes did not often go to school. If they did, they would attend a Dame school. Dame schools provided a basic education for girls. They were called 'Dame' schools because they were often run by a local, educated woman.

Women were not expected to go out into the world, but would go from being under their father's care to their husband's. They were not expected to support themselves. For most girls, education was focused on the home. As wives and mothers, they would need a wide variety of skills. For example, it was important to know how to preserve food, bake, brew, sew and treat simple ailments and injuries.

Labourers and poor children

Most Elizabethans, whether girls or boys, had no formal, school-based education, as the majority of the population were farmers or labourers. They learned what they needed from their families, working on the land or in the home. In most cases, children needed to contribute to the family income from as early an age as possible, and the jobs they could expect to find did not require literacy or numeracy.

For everyone in Elizabethan society, the education or training you received would fit you for the life you were expected to lead, depending upon your place in the social order.

How big an impact did schools have on Elizabethans?

It is estimated that around 30% of men and 10% of women were literate by the end of Elizabeth I's reign in 1603, compared with 20% of men and 10% of women in the 1530s. This suggests that there was an improvement in education for boys during Elizabethan times, but not for girls. Leading thinkers and writers increasingly believed in women having a good education. However, they were usually highly educated and well-off, and a main obstacle to schooling was its cost. There weren't only fees to consider, but the loss of family income from children not working.

This might explain why ordinary people's attitudes to educating their daughters does not seem to have changed in Elizabethan times. Girls were expected to marry, not to work outside the home. Boys were expected to find paid employment and support their wives and children. A little education could help them find a better job.

Education in universities

For those who were able to go on to higher education, Elizabethan England had two universities: Oxford and Cambridge. Unlike today, you would start university at about the age of 14 or 15. The curriculum included Geometry, Music, Astronomy, Philosophy, Logic and Rhetoric,* as well as Medicine, Law and Divinity. The highest university qualification was the doctorate. Doctorates could be taken in Medicine, Law or Divinity.

> ### Key term
>
> **Rhetoric***
> The art of public speaking and persuasion.

Oxford and Cambridge universities are made up of different colleges, many of which were founded by the Tudors. In 1571, Elizabeth I founded Jesus College in Oxford to educate Welsh boys. One of Elizabeth's Privy Councillors, Sir Walter Mildmay, founded Emmanuel College in Cambridge in 1584. Both Elizabeth and Mildmay wanted their colleges to educate more Protestant clergymen, so to increase the number of well-educated, Protestant clergymen.

In London, the Inns of Court trained lawyers. Some young men went to study and practise law at the Inns of Court, rather than Oxford or Cambridge, for their higher education.

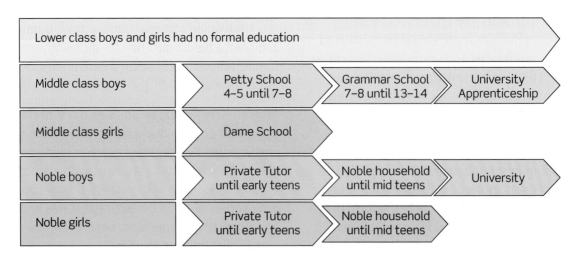

Figure 3.2 The different educational expectations of Elizabethan children according to gender and class.

Activities   ?

1. Draw up a chart to show the different education available to Elizabethans. There should be one column for girls and one for boys. There should be three rows: one for upper class children, one for well-off children and one for poor children. Make a note of what they learned, where and how long they would be in education.

2. Write a short paragraph explaining why education grew in Elizabethan times. Give examples of the types of schools and subjects that developed to support your points. You must include universities. For example, how did Protestantism encourage more education?

3. Why would Elizabeth I be so keen to educate more Protestant clergymen during her reign? What other events / issues was she dealing with in 1571 and 1584 that could help explain the founding of Jesus College Oxford and Emmanuel College Cambridge? Write a short paragraph discussing this question.

Leisure

As with many other aspects of life in Elizabethan England, your social class and gender could determine what sports and leisure activities you could participate in. The wealthier classes had much more opportunity to enjoy leisure pursuits. When it came to taking part in sports, there were more options for men than women.

Participation in leisure – sport

Nobility and gentry

Sports played by the nobility included:

- hunting on horseback, with hounds (both men and women)
- hawking (men and women)
- fishing (men and women)
- fencing (men)
- real tennis (men).

Source B

Real tennis, from a 16th-century engraving. Real tennis was an indoor game played by upper class men. It was a cross between modern tennis and squash. Balls could bounce off the walls as long as they did not do go above a certain limit, otherwise it was out.

Some sports were played by men of all social classes, although they would not take part together. Wrestling and swimming were popular with men of all classes. Noble men would wrestle in private; men of a lower social class would take part in public wrestling matches. Gambling on the outcome was very popular. The nobility and gentry would often bet and watch alongside the other classes.

Working people: craftsmen, farmers and labourers

Football was a lower class game for men. It was extremely violent. It was not unknown for men to be killed during matches, which could last for hours. The aim of the game was similar to football matches today: to get the ball into the other side's goal. However, unlike today, the goals themselves came in all shapes and sizes. Football did not resemble the modern game. There were no rules against:

- picking up the ball and running with it
- the number of players
- tripping up the opposing team's players
- the size of pitch.

Sometimes the streets were pitches, sometime it was the countryside between two opposing village teams.

In fact, there really were no rules. Because of the random nature of the pitches, there were no set positions.

Spectator sports

The Elizabethans enjoyed watching sporting competitions, such as wrestling or tennis, depending upon their class. Watching animals fight to the death was also considered entertainment and people of all classes would watch, even Elizabeth I. Often, large sums of money would be gambled on the outcomes.

Baiting

During a baiting, a bear would be chained to a post and dogs unleashed against it. Despite the bear's teeth being broken short so that they could not bite the dogs, many were killed as the bear lashed out with its claws or pinned them under their paws. Care was taken not to kill the bears, if possible, as they were very expensive.

Bear baiting was so popular in Elizabethan England that special arenas were built in London to house them. All classes of people enjoyed watching what they considered to be a sport, including the queen.

Bull baiting was also popular. Most towns had a bull ring. As bulls were neither rare nor expensive, the fight was to the death. Yet again, dogs were set upon a chained bull. The bull would use its horns to fight them off, sending the dogs flying into the air.

Cock-fighting

Cockerels are aggressive birds and when cock-fighting, were made to wear metal spurs to attack each other, as well as using their beaks. Many places, even small towns, had special arenas built for cock-fighting. Again, all classes enjoyed it and bet huge sums on the outcomes of the fights.

Baiting and cock-fighting were not approved of by all Elizabethans. Puritans especially disapproved of them, although not because they felt the animals were being mistreated. The main reason for their disapproval was that the fights were usually held on Sundays, which they considered to be a holy day.

Pastimes

Literature

There was a lot of new literature written during Elizabeth I's reign. History was a very popular subject, as were accounts of voyages of discovery, and translations of Latin and Greek classics. Medieval works such as Chaucer's *Canterbury Tales* were also popular.

The most popular form of creative writing were poetry and plays. Most well-educated people wrote poetry, including the queen. Theatre, meanwhile, was undergoing a revolution in Elizabeth I's reign.

Theatre

Theatre developed as a result of Protestantism, which influenced many aspects of Elizabethan life. At the start of Elizabeth's reign, **mystery plays** were the most common form of theatre. These plays brought the Bible and saints' stories to life for an audience. Some Protestants believed that the centuries-old plays were another way for the Catholic Church to control interpretations of the Bible.

Saints were an important part of the Catholic religion, and the plays kept their memories (and miracles) in the public imagination. Elizabeth was also concerned that they would encourage religious violence, so her government put a stop to them. Theatre instead turned to new, non-religious (secular) plays.

These secular plays were in great demand. They were more exciting than the older religious plays, as unlike Bible stories, the endings were not already known. Comedies were also popular (the Elizabethan sense of humour was rude and vulgar). The demand for theatre rocketed and theatre companies were formed across England. They were usually established and funded by members of the nobility. The Earl of Leicester had his own company called **Leicester's Men**, and in 1583, Elizabeth I established **The Queen's Men**.

The popularity of plays led to the first purpose-built theatres being constructed. Originally, plays were performed in the courtyards of inns that had high galleries surrounding them, so the audience looked down on the action. However, with so much money to be made, purpose-built theatres began to appear. Many of the theatres were built in London: the first purpose-built theatre was the **Red Lion** in Whitechapel, constructed in 1567. Others included the **Rose** in 1587, not far from where the modern reconstruction of Shakespeare's **Globe** theatre is today.

> ## Source C
>
> A play being staged in Shakespeare's 'Globe' theatre.
>
>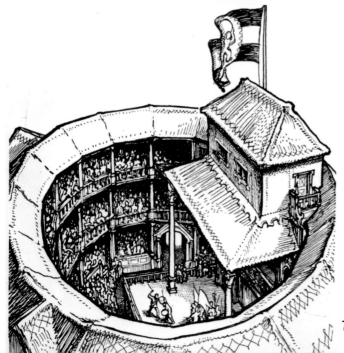

Theatre was popular with all classes. Well-known performers attracted large audiences. However, only men were allowed to act: women's parts were taken by boys. Sometimes there were queues of 2,000 people waiting to see a performance. Poor people could pay 1 penny to stand in the pit in front of the stage. The pit was an area in a theatre at the base of the stage.

Seats were very expensive. The most expensive place to sit was directly above the stage. This was not where the best view of the action was, but the important thing was to be seen sitting there by the rest of the audience.

Music and dancing

Elizabethans of all classes were passionate about music. Many people played instruments. Elizabethan instruments were not too different from those we have today: there were lutes (similar to guitars) and spinets and harpsichords (all similar to pianos). These were expensive instruments and would be found in noble and upper class households. Bagpipes and fiddles were especially popular with the lower classes.

Listening to music performances was also hugely popular. Wealthy families would employ their own musicians to play during meals and feasts, though only men could be paid musicians. The lower classes would listen to music at fairs, markets or on public occasions. Towns employed musicians to play at official functions or public events. There was music in church, taverns, barbers' shops and the streets. Books of popular songs could be bought.

New music was being composed to accompany the new secular plays in the theatre. There were also developments in musical instruments. This also contributed to more new music being composed and heard throughout England into Elizabeth's reign and beyond.

Dancing was very popular and, although upper and lower class people did not dance together, it did bring men and women together.

Interpretation 1 gives a very positive impression of life in Elizabethan England.

Interpretation 1

Historian Andrew Wilson interprets Elizabethan England as one which changed dramatically, in the book *The Elizabethans* (2011).

There were new schools… English ships – sailed to new lands, and brought back… the sense of an expanded world. In churches, halls, palaces and country houses, new music delighted the ear. You could not be alive in Elizabethan England and not feel that it was a young country, full of capacity to reinvent itself.

Activity

Work in groups of four. Two people should look for evidence that supports the idea of Elizabethan leisure pursuits as being positive, exciting and improving to us in the 21st century; two should look at evidence against. When you have finished, deliver a short presentation to show to the rest of the class what conclusions you have come to.

Summary

- Education expanded during Elizabeth I's reign, but this expansion was limited. Of those who did get an education, most were boys. The large majority of people were illiterate.
- There was not a great difference in the academic education of noble girls and boys. However, noble boys were expected to be much more active outside of the classroom.
- Every town in England had a grammar school by 1577.
- Elizabethan pastimes were similar to modern ones, but sport was much more violent.
- Theatre thrived: there were many new plays and purpose built theatres, and was popular with all classes in Elizabethan England.
- Protestantism led to the development of new plays.

Checkpoint

Strengthen

S1 Give two examples of Elizabethan schools and say who they were for.

S2 Why did education become more important in Elizabethan times?

S3 Give two examples of pastimes enjoyed by all Elizabethans.

Challenge

C1 Explain why literacy increased for males but not for females under Elizabeth's reign. Is this surprising, considering that England was under the rule of a young queen?

C2 What were the differences in pastimes between males and females?

C3 What were the differences in pastimes between rich and poor?

When answering C2 and C3, making a table listing all the differences you can think of may help in structuring your answers.

3.2 The problem of the poor

Learning objectives

- Understand the reasons why poverty and vagabondage increased in Elizabethan England.
- Understand how and why attitudes towards the poor shifted during Elizabeth's reign.

The main question to ask when reading the next section is: why was there an increase in poverty and vagabondage between 1558 and 1588?

Who were the poor?

For ordinary Elizabethans, not being able to work meant a life of poverty. Unemployment and illness could lead to starvation, as people did not have enough money to feed themselves or their families. Different people in different places would find themselves in poverty at different times in their lives.

Elizabethan society was concerned with those who were poor enough to need financial help (poor relief) or charity (alms), or who begged or were homeless. They were also concerned with 'itinerants' – people who had moved from their home parishes looking for work. Modern historians sometimes identify the 'poor' as those who spent 80% of their income on bread.

A survey of the poor in Norwich was undertaken in 1570. The city's mayor wanted to investigate how many 'itinerants' were renting rooms in Norwich, how long they had been living there, where they had come from, and their circumstances. They were looking for anyone who was receiving, or might in future need, poor relief.

The survey showed that 40% of the poor counted were under 16 years old. Families headed by women (often widows) also tended to be very poor, as women were paid a lot less than men if they had to work. Even families where there was an adult male in work could be so poor that 80% of their income simply went on buying enough food not to starve. Of all adults included, two-thirds were women and a quarter of those were over the age of 60. In many cases, these women had been abandoned by their husbands or were widows.

Why did poverty increase?

Population growth

During the reign of Elizabeth I, England's population grew by as much as 35%. This population growth was spread throughout the country, but towns and cities in particular grew especially fast. London became the fastest growing city in England: it had a population of 150,000 in 1603, ten times the size of England's second city, Norwich.

However, although the urban population of these growing towns and cities needed food, they didn't grow any themselves. Food was grown in the countryside and brought into urban areas for sale. Because there were more people to feed, the price of food in towns rose.

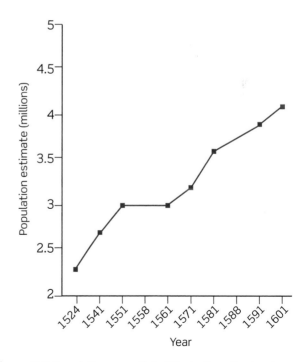

Figure 3.3 Population growth in Elizabethan England.

Rising prices

Prices of food rose even further when harvests were bad and there wasn't enough food to go around. Food production grew much more slowly than the population, despite books explaining ways to improve harvests being published. Bread was the basis of most people's diets, and grain prices rose fastest of all.

Poverty also increased because wages did not rise as fast as prices. With more people wanting work, labour was cheaper. Many landowners and employers cut wages to keep their costs down.

As the population grew, so did the demand for land. This meant that landowners could charge much higher rents for land where people lived or farmed. When someone took over a piece of land they also had to pay an **entry fee**. These went up, too. Some tenants could not afford to keep their land; others were evicted to make way for sheep farming.

Changes in the countryside: sheep farming

English wool and woollen cloth accounted for 81.6% of England's exports during Elizabeth's reign. The price of wool increased as demand for woollen cloth grew. This meant that farming sheep became very profitable and more landowners turned to it as a way to make money. However, it was a large-scale business that only larger farms could afford. It was not uncommon for flocks to

contain over 2,000 sheep. The increase in sheep farming was blamed for the problems because:

- sheep farming took land that had once been used for growing crops, or as **common land** (see below)
- farming sheep did not require as much labour as growing crops, so rural unemployment rose
- feeding sheep over winter meant that some crops were grown only for animals to eat. This angered many when large numbers of people were going hungry or could not afford bread.

Changes in the countryside: enclosure

Enclosing land meant replacing large, open fields that were farmed by villagers with individual fields belonging to one person. Enclosure also often led to small farms being merged and tenant farmers evicted. It also resulted in unemployment and rural depopulation*. Enclosure caused great anger and resentment.

Why did farmers enclose the land?

Farming techniques were improving in the 16th century. New ideas and good practice were spreading thanks to increasing numbers of printing presses. Some farmers began to control animal breeding to produce better livestock. Therefore, they needed to keep them in enclosed fields to stop them wandering off. Some farmers also benefitted from livestock being kept in enclosed fields, as it stopped them trampling other crops.

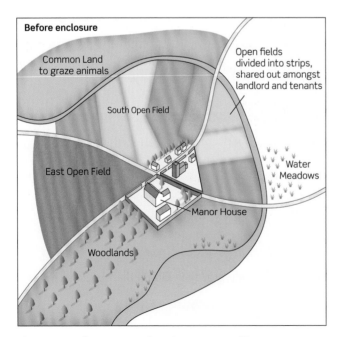
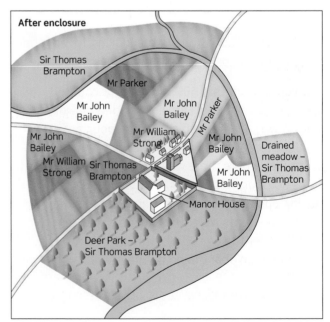

Figure 3.4 The impact of enclosure on a village.

Enclosing land was not just important for animal farmers. Rising food prices encouraged an increase in arable farming,* too. New farming techniques, such as improving land drainage and better use of fertiliser, also produced more crops. Enclosed fields were easier to drain and made planting and caring for larger crops easier.

Some farmers practised both arable and animal farming, known as 'up and down husbandry'. Land would be used for crops one year and livestock the next. The livestock fertilised the field so that when crops were planted the following year, the soil produced more.

However, for this to be effective, animals needed to be in enclosed fields so that the manure left by the animals was where it was needed. Before enclosure, when there were three large, open fields, one field was left **fallow** (unused) for a year to let the soil recover. This was not a good use of the land.

Key terms

Rural depopulation*
When the population of the countryside falls as people move away in search of a better life.

Arable farming*
Growing crops on farm land.

Why did enclosure cause poverty to increase?
Enclosure did not make landowners poor – they often grew rich. However, ordinary farm labourers, or those who could not afford increased rents, suffered.

More efficient techniques for growing crops led to fewer labourers being needed, which reduced landowners' costs. Sheep farming also required less labour than arable farming, as sheep did not need much looking after other than at lambing or shearing times. As the population rose and the supply of labour increased, wages were reduced, too.

Sometimes the common land in a village was enclosed. Common land was where people had ancient rights, so that they were free to graze their pigs, collect firewood or even forage for food. For those people who were

subsistence farming,* the common land was vital for survival. Enclosing common land, therefore, caused a great deal of anger and resentment. Interpretation 1 sees enclosure as being one of the most significant social problems of Elizabethan England.

Key term

Subsistence farming*
Growing just enough to feed the family but not to sell.

Interpretation 1

In Ian Mortimor's *The Time Traveller's Guide to Elizabethan England* (2013), changes to the countryside are described as being a great cause of strife.

… the destruction of arable fields and villages is a profound worry to the families who are evicted. It is equally worrying to the authorities in those towns where the homeless husbandmen [famers, land workers] go begging. The gradual loss of land to the working man and his family may fairly be described as the second-greatest single cause of unrest during the reign, second only to religion.

Land values and rents
As the money that could potentially be earned from farming increased, landowners put up the rents of tenant farmers. Those who could not pay were forced off the land to make way for wealthier, more successful tenants. Sometimes the land they vacated was enclosed instead.

How big was the problem of enclosure?
A pamphlet by Sir Thomas Smith, written in the 1560s, blamed gentry and yeomen for preferring sheep to crops because of better prices for wool. This led to a great deal of hostility towards those who owned sheep farms, especially where they took common land and **enclosed** it for their sheep. It was commonly felt that growing food for people should take priority.

In actual fact, only 2–3% of land in England was enclosed by the end of the 16th century. Where it took place, however, it had a great impact and there were plenty of commentators like Smith who wrote against it. Combined with rising food prices and an increasing numbers of vagabonds (see below) adding to unemployment in towns and cities, enclosure provided both a simple explanation for these problems and a scapegoat for the blame.

Reasons for the increase in vagabondage

Vagabondage was something that greatly concerned Elizabethans, especially the government and nobility. Elizabethan society had a strict hierarchy in which everyone had a place. Vagabonds* lived outside this hierarchy as they had no place – no employer, no master, no place where they belonged. They often lived outside the law, too. Therefore, Elizabethan society feared vagabonds as they threatened law and order.

The urban poor

Rural depopulation made the problem of vagabondage worse. Many people left their home villages to look for work in towns and cities. However, city life could be hard, especially when there was an economic recession*, for example when poor relations between England and Spain led to trade embargos with the Netherlands (see Chapter 2) and big increases in unemployment. This resulted in many people who had left their villages becoming beggars or turning to a life of crime. Outside London's city walls, the poor built shacks which were tightly packed together. As they were outside the city, they were outside the authority of government officials. Crime and disorder were rife. All towns faced similar problems.

The number of urban poor grew very fast. Until Elizabethan times, it was thought that people who were able to work (but didn't) were simply idle. Elizabeth I's government eventually came to recognise that unemployment was a genuine problem. In many places, there were not enough jobs. Nevertheless, they continued to treat vagrants harshly.

Key terms

Vagabonds*

Vagabonds, or vagrants, were homeless people without jobs, who roamed the countryside begging for money, perhaps stealing or committing other crimes in order to survive.

Economic recession*

When a fall in demand leads to falling prices and businesses losing money. This can lead to businesses failing and unemployment going up.

Activity ?

Create a flow chart to show how an increase in population led to rising prices, which in turn led to enclosure, then unemployment, vagabondage.

Changing attitudes and policies towards the poor

Impotent and able bodied poor

There was some financial help available for the very poor. This was known as **poor relief** and was paid for by a special local tax, the **poor rate**. Justices of the Peace (JPs) organised poor relief. For many Elizabethans, helping the less fortunate was a Christian duty. Individual charity was another source of help.

Although Tudor people were sympathetic towards those who were unable to work because of age or illness (known as the **impotent** or **deserving** poor), those who were fit to work but didn't (the **able bodied** or **idle** poor) were treated more harshly. Vagrants faced severe punishment if they were caught, such as whipping and imprisonment.

When trade was bad, especially the cloth trade, the numbers of people who were abled bodied poor increased more than ever before. This is not surprising, as England's population was growing. The problem of the able bodied poor was especially noticeable in towns because:

- the poor and unemployed were very visible in towns as there were so many of them
- many people who lost their livelihoods in rural areas came to towns in search of work.

The cloth trade was especially bad in the years 1563–64, 1568–73 and 1586–88. During Elizabeth's reign, therefore, unemployment became recognised as a real social and economic problem. This led to the development of new ways to help the poor. It is interesting to note that the key laws to help the poor were passed in 1563, 1572 and 1576, which was the year of the Spanish Fury (see page 55).

Source A

A vagrant is tied and whipped through the streets as punishment. This engraving is from 16th-century England.

Government action

Although poor relief was a local issue, dealt with in a variety of ways in different places, Elizabeth I's government also adopted a more national approach across the whole country. When Elizabeth came to the throne, local officials had the power to collect poor rates on a weekly basis, as necessary, and distribute it to the impotent poor. However, vagrants were whipped and expelled from the parish if they had not been born there.

New laws were passed by Elizabeth I's Parliament. The main reason for some of these particular Acts of Parliament was fear of vagrancy and social unrest. However, they also show changes in how the poor were seen, with unemployment being recognised as a problem that needed to be tackled. The 1572 Vagabonds Act was a turning point, as it established a national poor rate for the first time. It also recognised unemployment as a real problem, because it gave towns the responsibility of providing work to the able bodied poor rather than simply punishing them for their circumstances.

1563 Statute of Artificers	1572 Vagabonds Act	1576 Poor Relief Act
Aim: to ensure that poor relief was collected. Features: • anyone who refused to pay the poor rates could be imprisoned • officials failing to organise poor relief could be fined up to £20.	Aim: to deter vagrancy. Features: • the Act stated that vagrants were to be whipped and a hole drilled through each ear • vagrants were also to be imprisoned if arrested a second time for vagrancy, and given the death penalty for the third. Also: • it established the national poor rate for the first time. This sheltered the impotent poor • JPs were to keep a register of the poor • towns and cities were given the responsibility to find work for the able bodied poor.	Aim: to distinguish between able bodied and impotent poor, and to help the able bodied poor find work. Features: • JPs provided the able bodied poor with wool and raw materials to enable them to work by making things to sell • those who refused work where they were given help to be sent to a special prison funded by poor rates, known as the house of correction.

The impact of the Elizabethan poor laws

Although there were changes for the better, poverty continued to be a major problem throughout Elizabeth I's reign. This was because of the conflict with Spain and the revolt in the Netherlands, which hit trade in England badly. Pamphlet writers stirred up fear of vagabonds, as more and more people appeared in towns and cities looking for work. Although they were a real problem, ordinary Elizabethans were often sympathetic. Some local records show that less than 10% of vagrants were whipped in some towns. In most cases, they were given money and sent on their way. This was often cheaper for the parish than whipping the vagrants and sending them back to their home parish.

The most important change to Elizabethan poor laws was the recognition of unemployment as a genuine problem: it was not simply laziness. Providing the poor with a way to make things to sell became the law across England. This helped the unemployed keep some independence and dignity, and often enabled them to stay in their home town or village. It formed an important part of poor relief until the 19th century.

Exam-style question, section B

Describe **two** features of the Elizabethan system of poor relief that were new. **4 marks**

Exam tip

The word 'new' is very important. You won't be awarded marks for writing about things that stayed the same in Elizabethan times.

There were still local differences in the way in which the poor were treated. Ipswich, especially, was ahead of much of the rest of England when it came to poor relief. As early as 1569, it had established a school for poor children and a hospital for those who were poor because they were sick. They had also made a special prison for the idle poor. In some London parishes, special help was provided for abandoned babies, the old and the sick.

Summary

- Poverty and vagabondage were seen as growing problems in Elizabethan England.
- The Elizabethans generally divided the poor into categories: the 'idle' and 'deserving', or 'impotent'.
- Population growth was one of the main reasons for the increase in poverty.
- Enclosure, disruptions to trade and inflation also led to the increase in poverty.
- Attitudes to the poor changed as unemployment became recognised as a genuine issue.
- Elizabeth I's government passed parliamentary laws to tackle poverty and vagabondage.
- One change was that local officials were to provide raw materials, such as wool, for the unemployed so that they could make things to sell.
- Vagabonds faced harsh punishments, although few local authorities actually applied them.
- There were local initiatives to help the poor as well, especially in towns like Ipswich.

Checkpoint

Strengthen

S1 Give two reasons why poverty increased in Elizabethan times.

S2 Explain why vagabondage increased in Elizabethan times.

S3 Describe one positive change in how Elizabethans treated the poor.

S4 Identify one Elizabethan Poor Law and say what it did to help the poor.

Challenge

C1 Explain the importance of the following when discussing the increase in Elizabethan poverty: enclosure; disruption to trade; population growth.

C2 Can you identify one key turning point in the treatment of the poor and explain why it was so important?

C3 Can you identify and explain a reason why some treatments of the poor did not change under Elizabeth's reign?

Make sure you understand the definitions of important terms used in this section, such as 'vagabondage' and 'poverty', before answering these questions.

3.3 Exploration and voyages of discovery

What led Elizabethans to explore?

Expanding trade

Trade was expanding rapidly as the New World began to open up new opportunities. English merchants needed to look for more new trading opportunities, as conflict with Spain and in the Netherlands had hit the traditional wool and cloth trade hard. As England relied upon its exports of cloth so much, it was vital to find new markets and new products to sell. Reports from the Americas suggested that there was an abundance of different crops, animal skins and precious metals.

Private investors, including Elizabeth I and her courtiers, funded many of the voyages of discovery. Although it was risky, the rewards could be enormous. Spain was certainly becoming very rich thanks to its silver mines in Peru, as well as the export of exotic crops such as sugar cane and tobacco. The vast majority of the Americas was undiscovered and there were hopes of finding even more riches away from the coasts, where there had been little exploration.

The Triangular Trade

Slavery has existed for thousands of years across all continents, societies and cultures. During Elizabeth I's reign, English merchants first began to exploit the ancient African slave trade. It eventually developed on a massive, trans-Atlantic scale, with the buying, or seizing, of hundreds of Africans to ship to the New World. It caused untold misery to the many and made huge fortunes for the few.

John Hawkins was a navigator, slave trader and the man behind some of the key developments in the English navy that enabled the Armada to be defeated (see page 61). He first bought slaves from Africa in 1562, transported them across the Atlantic and sold them to the Spanish colonists. He bought ginger, animal hides, sugar and pearls with some of the proceeds, making a huge profit and repeating the journey in 1564. This helped to lay the foundations of the infamous **Triangular Trade**.

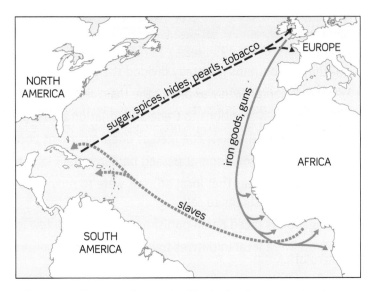

Figure 3.5 The early Triangular Trade that began to develop after John Hawkins' 1561–62 voyage.

New Technology

Navigation

Navigation was becoming increasingly more precise. For example, by 1584, the English mathematician Thomas Harriot worked out a simpler way of using the Sun to calculate the true sailing direction of a ship. This made voyages safer, more direct and faster. Other mathematical methods of navigation were also figured out and published in books.

Since the 15th century, quadrants* and astrolabes* had been increasingly used to make more accurate calculations about a ship's position. They used the position of the stars to do this. Making navigation simpler and more accurate was vital for long voyages of discovery. These journeys were sometimes recorded, making it easier for others to follow the routes mapped out. Printed books detailing voyages were becoming increasingly available.

Source A

An illustration from a 1551 French sailing manual showing how to use an astrolabe.

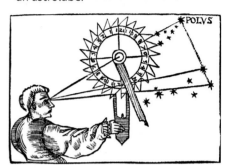

Key terms

Quadrant*

Similar to an astrolabe, it was used by sailors to help with navigation at sea. It was the shape of a quarter circle.

Astrolabe*

An instrument used by sailors to help with navigation at sea. It was circular.

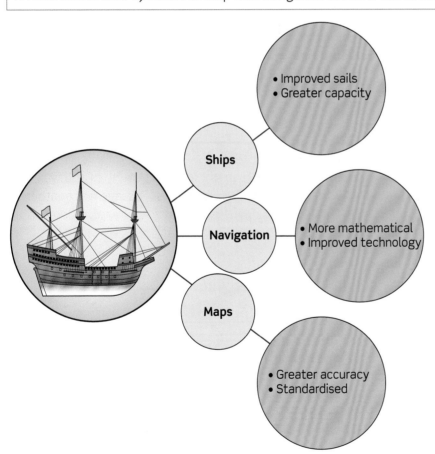

- Improved sails
- Greater capacity

Ships

Navigation

- More mathematical
- Improved technology

Maps

- Greater accuracy
- Standardised

Figure 3.6 Improved technology on ships during Elizabeth's reign.

Maps

Improved navigation and records of voyages contributed to more accurate maps. In 1569, the **Mercator map** was developed by the cartographer (map maker) Gerardus Mercator. He used parallel and evenly spaced lines of **longitude** and **latitude** to place lands more accurately on a map. Sailors now had a much more realistic picture of the world to use when plotting voyages. Printing also enabled these maps to become more widespread and consistent between different copies. Previously, maps had been copied and hand drawn, which lead to a lot of mistakes and inconsistencies.

Source B

A world map made by Gerardus Mercator, printed in 1587. The world's geography is clearly recognisable.

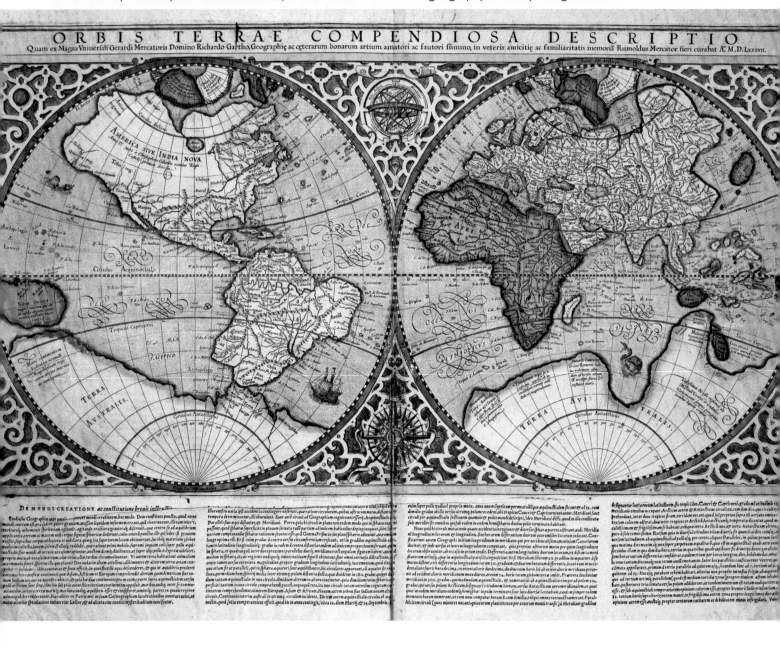

Ship design

Larger, more stable ships

Ship design improved, making longer journeys possible.

Galleons were developed in the 16th century. Galleons were ships that were much larger than traditional trading ships, which meant larger cargoes could be stowed in them. Galleons enabled more supplies to be taken on board, essential for long journeys across the Atlantic and Pacific oceans. This made them useful for both trade and voyages of discovery. Another design improvement was that, previously, ships had high, built up **bows** and **sterns** known as 'castles' – the fore and the aftcastles. On galleon ships, these were lowered, making the ship more stable in heavy seas. (See Figure 3.7.)

Faster, more manoeuvrable ships

Galleons also used different sail types on the same vessel: traditional square sails for speed on the bowsprit, fore and main masts; and Lateen (triangular) sails on the mizzen-mast, making them easier to manoeuvre. More masts and sails enabled longer, faster and more accurate voyages. Figure 3.7 shows the various parts of the ship.

Better fire power

Another important development concerning galleons was that they had gun decks running the length of the ship. Cannon could therefore fire from the sides as well as the bow and stern. This was important, as piracy was common, so ships often had to defend themselves. English and Spanish ships often attacked each other, too.

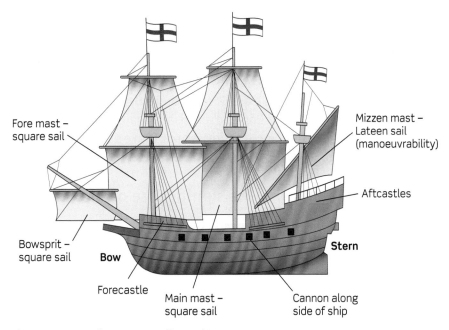

Fore mast – square sail

Mizzen mast – Lateen sail (manoeuvrability)

Aftcastles

Bowsprit – square sail

Bow

Forecastle

Main mast – square sail

Cannon along side of ship

Stern

Figure 3.7 A 16th-century galleon ship.

Drake's circumnavigation of the globe

Drake's circumnavigation of the globe took almost three years, from December 1577 until September 1580. Following this achievement, he was knighted by Elizabeth I.

Why did Drake circumnavigate the globe?

Drake had not set out with the aim of being the first Englishman to sail around the world. His main purpose was to raid Spanish colonies* in the Pacific. Relations with Spain were deteriorating at this time and this appears to have been upmost in the queen's mind.

Interpretation 1 suggests that Elizabeth I was not alone in wanting revenge on the Spanish. By 1578, relations between England and Spain were poor, and getting worse (see page 56). Drake also wanted revenge. In 1567–68, he had accompanied John Hawkins on a third trans-Atlantic expedition. This time the Spanish, angered at English attempts to break Spain's trading monopoly* in the New World, were prepared for battle. The English were attacked at St Juan de Ulúa. Their fleet was devastated and 325 of their sailors were killed. Forced to abandon some of his remaining men, Hawkins and Drake returned home with only 15 sailors.

> ### Key terms
>
> **Colonies***
>
> Lands under the control or influence of another country, occupied by settlers from that country.
>
> **Monopoly***
>
> When one person, or company, controls the supply of something. This means they can charge whatever price they like for it.

Interpretation 1

C.E. Hamshere plays down the significance of Drake's circumnavigation of the globe as a happy accident in the book *Drake's Voyage Around the World* (1967).

What is fairly evident is that Drake did not set out to perform the feat of circumnavigation. He probably carried the possibility in the back of his mind, but his prime object was to plunder the Spaniards, not to make a voyage of exploration. The discoveries he did make were incidental.

Although Drake and Elizabeth had political reasons for (what turned out to be) the circumnavigation, there were still great profits to be made from the journey into the Americas, and there were plenty of people willing to invest in his expedition at court. Despite the long and difficult voyage, Drake returned to England a rich, and famous, man. He also made his investors very rich. Some estimates put Drake's treasure haul at £500,000,000 in today's money!

What was the significance of Drake's circumnavigation?

England as a great sea-faring nation

Drake's voyage almost ended in disaster. He set out with five ships and, by the time he had reached the Pacific in 1578, he had only one left: the *Golden Hind*. One sailor, Captain Thomas Doughty, was executed on the voyage. Doughty had been accused of mutiny by Drake.

Despite this, he and his 56 surviving men managed to return to England in 1580 after circumnavigating the globe. They were only the second crew in history to have achieved such a feat. This was a great boost to English morale and established the reputation of English ships and sailors as being among the finest in the world. This was important at a time of growing fears that the Spanish could invade England at any time.

Activities ?

1   List as many reasons as you can why voyages of exploration were so dangerous.

2   Pick two reasons and describe why they made voyages of exploration so dangerous. Aim to write 50 words on each. Try to include some facts and examples in your answers.

Encouraging explorations

Drake and his crew survived in part by raiding Spanish ships and colonies up the coast of South America. How far north they then travelled has been debated, but it is believed that they made it as far north as Vancouver. They gathered a great deal of useful information about the Americas, as well as keeping thorough logs of their voyage that could be written up and shared with other English sailors.

Extend your knowledge

Davy Ingram

One of the most famous accounts of the Americas was written by Davy Ingram. He survived the Spanish attack on Drake and Hawkins at San Juan de Ulúa in Mexico and walked 3,000 miles north up the Atlantic coast of America. He told fantastical tales of great wealth to be found, including precious metals (buckets made of silver, great lumps of gold), minerals, fertile soil and bright red sheep and rabbits. Ingram also wrote about ritualistic cannibalism being practised by the Native Americans who, he claimed, killed and ate their sick – although they were very friendly to visitors. These tales encouraged more voyages of exploration.

Nova Albion

In June 1579, the *Golden Hind* was in urgent need of repair after having explored the furthest reaches of North America's Pacific coast. Drake landed in a bay that was probably north of modern day San Francisco. The local Native Americans treated the English with great hospitality. They performed a ceremony that Drake took to be the equivalent of a coronation. He therefore named the region **Nova Albion** and declared Elizabeth I to be its sovereign.

Elizabeth I and other European rulers did not recognise the agreement made by the pope almost a century earlier that gave the Americas to the Spanish and Portuguese. Elizabeth herself gave her explorers the right to take any land that no other Christian leader had claimed. The existing rights of the Native Americans (already living there) to the land were not considered. The peaceful welcome given to Drake in what was later called California encouraged the idea that Europeans could settle, and even rule, there.

Encouraging colonies in America

Although there were already plans being made to establish English colonies in the Americas, by the early 1570s, they had come to nothing. In 1578, while Drake was undertaking his circumnavigation, Elizabeth I gave Sir Humfrey Gilbert permission to set out on a voyage of discovery to North America. It ended in disaster. Gilbert was bankrupted. Yet in 1583, he was prepared to set out again. Since Gilbert's earlier failure, Drake had returned to England with wealth and reports that encouraged adventurers and investors to continue trying to establish their own colonies there.

Anglo–Spanish damaged relations

Drake was correct when he said that attacking Spain's American colonies would anger Philip II. The following year, Elizabeth I knighted Drake on the *Golden Hind*. This sent a clear message to Philip II. He regarded Drake as a pirate and Elizabeth's provocative actions as scandalous. It was one more event in deteriorating Anglo–Spanish relations.

Activities

1   List all the positives and negatives that you can find that happened during and after Drake's circumnavigation of the globe.

2   Use your list to explain why Elizabeth I knighted Drake on board the Golden Hind in 1581.

3   Imagine that you are a sailor having returned from Drake's circumnavigation of the globe. Write some diary entries about what has happened and why this journey was so important. Use the information here and research more of your own. You need to write at least three entries, but no more than five. You should say why the journey has been so hard, what happened to the other ships, what the high points of the voyage were and what happened in June 1579. To give extra details for your account, you could research the lands visited by Drake, what Francis Drake was really like or life at sea in Elizabethan times.

Summary

- Trade was the driving force behind voyages of exploration.
- Undermining Spain's position in the New World was another important reason for voyages of exploration, especially as Anglo–Spanish relations were getting worse.
- New technology made ships more capable of undertaking longer journeys.
- New technology also led to more accurate maps and navigation.
- Printing enabled the reproduction of standardised maps, navigation manuals and accounts of the fabulous riches to be found in the New World, encouraging more exploration.
- Drake's circumnavigation of the globe began as a mission to attack Spanish colonies.
- Nova Albion encouraged the English to attempt the further colonisation of North America.
- Drake's circumnavigation was extremely profitable and encouraged more investment in voyages of explorations.

Checkpoint

Strengthen

S1 Give two reasons why there were voyages of exploration during Elizabeth I's reign.

S2 How did improved technology help encourage long voyages?

S3 Give one reason why Drake circumnavigated the globe 1577–80.

S4 Give one consequence of Drake's circumnavigation of the globe.

Challenge

C1 Which technological development do you consider most important to encouraging voyages of exploration and why?

C2 Explain why Drake's circumnavigation of the globe encouraged **both** exploration **and** the colonisation of America.

If you are not confident about any of these questions, form a group with other students, discuss the answers and then record your conclusion. Your teacher can give you some hints.

3.4 Raleigh and Virginia

Learning objectives

- Understand the significance of the attempts to colonise Virginia.
- Understand why the attempts to colonise Virginia failed.

Timeline
The colonisation of Virginia

1578 Sir Humfrey Gilbert sets out to North America on voyage of exploration but fails and is bankrupted

1580 Drake returns from circumnavigating the globe with spices, treasure and tales of Nova Albion

1583 Gilbert leads another voyage of exploration to America. It fails. Gilbert dies on the return journey

1584 Raleigh begins planning new colonisation attempt by sending a fact-finding mission to Virginia

1585 Colonists set sail for North America and begin the English colonisation of Virginia

1586 Surviving colonists abandon Virginia and return to England

1587 New group of colonists arrive in Virginia and establish colony at Roanoke

1590 English sailors arrive at Roanoke only to find it abandoned. All the colonists have disappeared

Key term

Barter*
Exchanging goods for other goods, instead of paying for something outright.

Walter Raleigh's significance

Walter Raleigh was born into a gentry's family. He became an explorer and courtier during the reign of Elizabeth I. He was also a writer and historian, and is associated with popularising tobacco in England.

In 1584, Walter Raleigh was given a grant from Elizabeth I to explore and settle in lands in North America. There had already been two failed attempts (see the timeline to the left). Because of these failures, it made any new projects attempting the same thing even harder. Raleigh needed to raise huge amounts of money and encourage potential English colonists to leave their homes and settle in a land many knew little about.

Raleigh did not lead the colonists to Virginia himself. Elizabeth I did not want to lose one of her favourite courtiers whilst there was still a concern over Anglo–Spanish relations. However, he was very significant because he:

- investigated, organised and raised funds for the establishment of an English colony in Virginia
- promoted the voyage and persuaded people to leave England and settle in Virginia
- appointed the governor of Virginia, who ruled in his place
- developed a 'blueprint' that was to be used for later English colonisations.

Investigating and promoting the Virginia project

Raleigh sent a fact-finding expedition to Virginia in 1584. The explorers who went were able to barter* tin utensils and metal knives (Native American knives were wooden) for game, fish, nuts and a variety of fruits and vegetables. The Indians were very friendly and welcoming to the English. The accounts brought back to England described this part of North America as a paradise.

Raleigh used these findings to persuade a group of English men to leave their homes and make the dangerous voyage across the Atlantic. They were convinced that they would find their fortunes in Virginia. This was important because the first expeditions had not been successful and in London, other travellers had spread rumours of fantastical monsters and brutal savages in America.

Manteo and Wanchese

The 1584 expedition also brought two Native American Indians, Manteo and Wanchese, back to England. They were very useful. Thomas Harriot, a mathematician, learned their language (Algonquian), and taught them English. He was then able to make an English–Algonquian 'dictionary'. Manteo and Wanchese also helped the first English colonists to establish contact with their people.

Raising funds

The cost of the colonisation project was enormous – there was not enough money to successfully colonise in the New World by just trading on the voyage. However, there were clear economic benefits to be had that made the voyage worthwhile.

- Native Americans would barter things for simple, cheap English goods like woollen cloth.
- The colony would provide work for English cloth makers and merchants.
- The colony could provide exotic materials such as gold and tobacco that could be brought back to England.
- Because of these gains, there would be plenty of revenues for the English government.

Raleigh hoped that the government would fund the new colony. The queen refused. Elizabeth was notoriously careful with money, and had other financial concerns at the time, such as the threat from Spain. She did, however, suggest that the land colonised be called Virginia in her honour (the 'Virgin Queen'). She also gave him a ship and gunpowder worth £400. Raleigh was one of Elizabeth I's favourites, and this royal backing gave the project prestige. It helped to encourage others to invest, especially courtiers like Sir Francis Walsingham.

Raleigh promised investors that he would take any Spanish ships that he came across, including their cargoes. This was important in encouraging merchants to invest. They had already seen how much Drake had brought back from the Americas in 1580.

Raleigh also invested a lot of his own money in the venture. This was important if others were to believe that it could work. By 1585, he had the resources he needed.

Extend your knowledge

The Algonquian people

The Indians in the region that the English wanted to settle were mainly Algonquian. They shared a common language and culture. Each settlement (the equivalent of an English town) had a Chief. Paramount Chiefs then ruled two or more of these settlements. The English expedition in 1584 met a local Paramount Chief, Wingina, who ruled several small settlements on Roanoke Island. The popular idea that all Native Americans were simple, often aggressive, tribes with very little structure or government is misleading. The Algonquian people had their own political system, culture and laws. The English colonists who expected to be able to take over and govern not only the land, but its people, were disappointed. They needed to work with, rather than rule, the Native Americans. This was not what they expected.

Who?

- Hopefully about 300 colonists (must have a variety of skills)
- Landowners, farmers and artisans (e.g. blacksmiths, carpenters, bottle makers, stone-masons, weavers, tanners, cobblers)
- Hunters (and hunting dogs) and fishermen
- Clergy
- Soldiers to protect the other colonists
- Make sure there are enough farmers to feed the artisans, clergy and others.

Supplies?

- Enough food to get across the Atlantic and last until harvest
- Fresh water for the voyage
- Tools and raw materials for the artisans
- Farming implements
- Seeds for planting
- Weapons
- Salt for preserving food

When to sail?

- Must set sail in enough time for sowing crops (good harvest essential to see the colonists through the winter)
- **but** they can't go without enough colonists of the right kind

Ships?

- Sufficient ships that are big enough to carry colonists and supplies
- Well armed, in case of attack by Spanish or pirates

Other considerations

- Spain controls the Caribbean and Florida, so colonists could be attacked
- Will need to buy animals in the Caribbean, for eating and breeding
- Building shelter – including a fort – when they have arrived
- Variety of seeds and in huge quantities (until enough can be grown for some more to be used as seed)
- Colonists will need to barter with Indians when they first arrive
- The Queen says I can't go: who will lead the voyage and the colony?
- Will need to raise a **lot** of money!

Figure 3.8 Raleigh's organisations and planning to prepare for the voyage to Virginia.

Organising the Virginia project

Finding colonists and sailors

Finding colonists and sailors willing to cross the Atlantic was difficult. In the end, Raleigh's colony had only 107 colonists, rather than the 300 he had hoped. They were all men. Almost half were soldiers, but there were landowners, farmers, skilled craftsmen (artisans) and also a mathematician. Many were attracted by the promise of making their fortune in Virginia.

Appointing leaders

Raleigh was not allowed to lead the expedition himself. Elizabeth I considered it too dangerous to risk her favourite courtier who was, in any case, needed in England as fear of a Spanish invasion grew. The table below shows the men chosen by Raleigh for the job.

Who	Role	Suitability
Richard Grenville	Expedition commander	Grenville was a very experienced sailor and soldier; adventurous and hot headed. He did not get on with Ralph Lane, the governor of Virginia. He was known to be feared rather than loved.
Ralph Lane	Governor of Virginia	Lane was an expert on fort building. He was also an explorer and a battle hardened soldier who could rise to a challenge. He enjoyed hardship and pitting his wits against nature with his 'can do' attitude.
Thomas Harriot	Translator and cartographer	Harriot had worked with Manteo and Wanchese, the Native Americans brought to England in 1584 to learn Algonquin, with whom he formed a strong bond. He understood navigation and was skilled at making maps.

Ships and timing

Raleigh sent five ships to Virginia: *Tiger*, *Roebuck*, *Lion*, *Dorothy* and *Elizabeth*. The *Tiger* was the largest and carried all the perishables – meats, vegetables, beer, wine, seeds and grain for bread. The ships left England on 9 April 1585. With a journey of several weeks ahead of them, this was already too late for planting some of their crops needed to see them through the winter.

The English landed on Roanoke Island in late 1585. This, and the surrounding areas, was where the English colonists first settled.

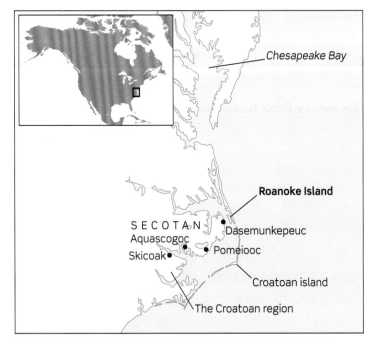

Figure 3.9 Roanoke Island and the surrounding area, where the English colonists first settled.

Why was the colonisation of Virginia significant?

Undermining Spain

One of the main reasons why the colonisation of Virginia at this time was significant was because it provided England with a base from which to attack Spanish colonies in the New World. Virginia was ideally placed – not too far from Florida and the Caribbean for attacks to be launched, but far enough away to be reasonably safe from the Spanish.

Interpretation 1

Kupperman puts much score in privateering as a reason for Elizabethan colonisation in the book *Roanoke* (2007).

The desire to establish colonies in America was inseparable in these early years from privateering. When Raleigh decided to found the colony at Roanoke, his major reason was that it could serve as a base for privateering.

So, the early colonisation of North America was part of the England's conflict with Spain, but not just for the short term. In the longer term, England hoped to rival Spain's overseas empire and undermine its influence in the New World. A successful colony in Virginia would serve as an example for other ventures. It would also offer the Native Americans an alternative to Spanish domination: they could choose to turn to English settlers for trade instead, or to help them against the Spanish.

The roots of the British Empire

In the next century, the English did indeed succeed in establishing a strong presence in North America. Although these early attempts to settle in Virginia failed (as explained below), they did provide an opportunity to learn from the mistakes they made. The roots of the British Empire that developed in the 18th and 19th centuries can be found in these 16th-century experiments on settling in new and foreign lands.

Economic benefits

Trade was vital to the English economy. Elizabeth I had hoped to encourage English merchants to find new markets as the conflict with Spain made trading in Europe increasingly difficult.

Relying on the Netherlands as England's main market and trade route was far too risky by the 1560s.

Many of the things that were supplied from southern Europe and the Mediterranean could be provided from Virginia. If England could control it, it would not be dependent upon countries like Spain, the Italian states and France for fruit, vines, spices and other luxuries. Tobacco is probably the most famous new crop and trade opportunity brought to England. It was popularised at court by Walter Raleigh. Sugar cane was another valuable crop to come from this part of America.

Why did the attempts to colonise Virginia fail?

There were **two** attempts at colonising Virginia at this time. Both failed. The fate of the 1587–90 colonisation is still a mystery, but the first colony failed for a number of reasons.

The voyage

On the first voyage to Virginia, the colonists left England too late to reach Virginia in time to plant crops. Also, before the colonists arrived, many were ill. The climate was hot, humid and mosquitoes were everywhere. Because of this, the food rotted quickly.

Disaster struck when the *Tiger* became damaged. A breach in the hull let in seawater that ruined the food it was carrying, including seeds for planting. The dried peas and beans were rescued and were edible, but they couldn't be planted. In any case, they had arrived too late to plant their own crops. Any hope of establishing a self-sufficient colony had been lost. The colonists were now dependent upon the Native Americans for food.

Colonists: expectations and reality

The colonists soon realised that the idyllic descriptions and reports of Virginia they had been given in England were far from the reality. Many merchants had come in the hope of getting rich quickly rather than being prepared to put in the necessary groundwork for establishing a working colony. They had hoped to find precious metals, but there were none. Being faced with the prospect of foraging for nuts and berries when the winter came was not what these men had signed up for.

Interpretation 2

Milton's interpretation below, from *Big Chief Elizabeth* (2000), suggests that the colonists themselves were the main reason for the colony's failure.

> But unbeknown to either the Spanish or the English, Ralph Lane's settlers were proving more than capable of destroying themselves.

The colonists did not co-operate effectively either. The merchants and 'gentlemen' amongst them had no intention of doing any physical work. They had expected to use Native Americans as labour, but they soon realised that ruling over the native people easily would be impossible. Those colonists who were farmers were not prepared to do the work for upper classes. They had not left England to become labourers, but to work their **own** land.

The soldiers who had volunteered for the voyage were important when defending the colony and leading expeditions to explore uncharted territory, but they did not have the skills to farm the land. They were also ill-disciplined. At least one soldier was executed and his body left rotting as a warning to others.

The colonists had a good skills base between them, but this added to the problems. There were too many craftsmen and not enough farmers. Many artisans, for example bakers, weavers and brewers, did not have the necessary raw materials. There also wasn't stone for the stonemasons, which meant that a planned fort could not be built as planned. Instead, it was built using wood.

Exam-style question, Section B

'The main reason that voyages of exploration were undertaken during Elizabeth I's reign was to increase England's wealth'. How far do you agree?

You may use the following in your answer:

- Anglo–Spanish relations
- developing trade.

You **must** also use information of your own. **16 marks**

Exam tip

You can make a link between developing trade and Anglo–Spanish relations, which were worsening. Remember, much of Spain's wealth was from its colonies in the New World.

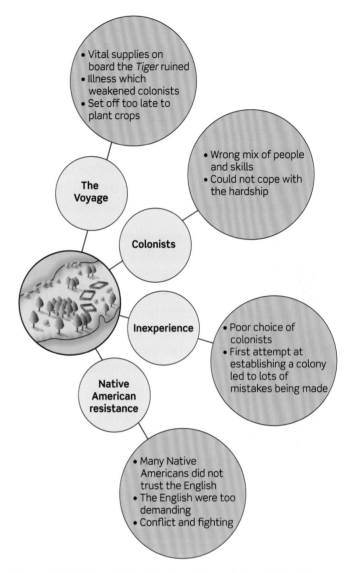

Figure 3.10 Why did the Virginia Colony fail in 1585–86?

The hunters and fishermen also faced problems. Most of the gunpowder was spoiled when the *Tiger* damaged its hull and so shooting game like pigeon and deer was very difficult. English fishing techniques did not work in the shallow waters around Roanoke Island.

Inexperience

Overall, therefore, the colonists were very reliant on the Native Americans for their survival. To some extent, the expedition's problems stemmed from it being the first ever undertaking of its kind by the English. Although Raleigh clearly tried to think of everything necessary for a thriving colony, there were not the right kinds of people in the right numbers. Before a colony thrives, it has to be established, and that is tough. Many were not cut out for a life of hardship and long-term rewards.

Native American resistance

The colonists were lucky to have Manteo and Wanchese with them to help establish relations with the Algonquian people. However, it was not enough. The local Chief, Wingina, ruled Roanoke Island and a small settlement on the mainland. He was an unpredictable character and suspicious of the English. He also grew tired of the constant demands for food handouts from the settlers. Although welcoming at first, Wingina turned against the English settlers.

Wingina believed that the English had supernatural powers from their God that they directed against the Native Americans. Many believed this because the English seemed to have the power to kill them without touching them: it was noticed that after the English left a settlement, many natives would die from strange causes they had never seen before. These were actually diseases brought from England that the natives had not encountered before.

There were also some violent clashes between the natives and English as the hardships of winter set in and the colonists wanted more handouts. By spring 1586, Wingina asked other chiefs to join with him to attack the English. Lane found out about the planned ambush, and was prepared. Wingina was killed. What happened next

Source A

A painting of one of the Indian settlements. It is Secotan in Virginia c1590. It was painted by John White, an artist sent to Virginia by Walter Raleigh.

is unknown, as the only document recording the event is Lane's journal and it has pages missing. However, records do show that he decided the colony had reached crisis point. Lane and the remaining colonists left Virginia and arrived back in Portsmouth on 27 July 1586.

Activity ?

How many examples of bad luck can you find in the section above that help to explain why the 1585 colonisation didn't work?

Extend your knowledge

Thomas Harvey and Thomas Harriot

The colonists who returned to England in 1586 were angry. They said they had been deceived by the promises about Virginia. They were especially scathing about the gentlemen and the colony's leaders. One, Thomas Harvey, was virtually bankrupted and taken to court over his debts. He used his trial to publicise his outrage. Thomas Harriot wrote a book to counter this. Called *A Briefe and True Report on America*, it painted a glossy picture of what Virginia had to offer.

Roanoke 1587–90

Despite the outcome of the first settlement, another attempt at colonising Virginia set out from England in 1587. This time there were 17 women and several families on board. Many colonists came from London's poverty-stricken alleys. They would be familiar with hardship and willing to work hard for a better life in the New World. Each was guaranteed to be given at least 500 acres of land to farm.

Manteo was made Lord of Roanoke by Walter Raleigh and the artist, John White, was put in overall charge of the expedition. White had already survived the 1585 colonisation and knew what to expect; Manteo might be able to encourage local Indians to co-operate with the English more. However, the Indians were hostile from the start.

John White's adviser, George Howe, disappeared. He was found dead. He had 16 arrow wounds. Manteo led an attack against the local Roanoke Indians as a retaliation, but it was a mistake: they killed some of the remaining friendly Indians from nearby Croatoan settlements instead.

John White was asked to go back to England to update Raleigh on what had happened. When he returned to Roanoke, three years later in 1590, it was deserted. What happened to the settlement remains a mystery. It is thought that hurricanes might have destroyed it, but this does not explain the fate of the colonists. The word **Croatoan** was found carved on a post. This suggested that they had relocated to the nearby Croatoan settlement. However, no trace of the colonists was ever found.

THINKING HISTORICALLY Cause and Consequence (3c&d)

Causation and intention

1 Work on your own or with a partner to identify as many causes of the failure of the Virginia colony in 1585–86 as you can. Write each cause on a separate card or piece of paper.

2 Divide your cards into those that represent:
    a the actions or intentions of people
    b the beliefs held by people at the time
    c the contextual factors, e.g. political, social or economic events
    d states of affairs (long-term situations that have developed over time).

3 Focus on the intentions and actions of the key people in the run-up to final failure of the Virginia colony in spring 1586: Sir Walter Raleigh, Ralph Lane, Chief Wingina, a gentleman colonist. For each person, draw on your knowledge to fill in a table, identifying:
    a their intentions in 1585
    b the actions they took to achieve these
    c the consequences of their actions (both intended and unintended)
    d the extent to which their intentions were achieved.

4 Discuss the following questions with a partner:
    a Did any one party intend for the Virginia colony to fail in spring 1586?
    b How important are people's intentions in explaining the failure of the Virginia colony in spring 1586?

Summary

- Walter Raleigh was behind two attempts to establish an English colony in Virginia.
- England's colonies in Roanoke failed due to inexperience, the suitability of the colonists and the resistance of local American Indians.
- Conditions in Virginia were much harsher than the colonists were expecting.
- Many of the 1585 colonists did not co-operate with each other.
- The English were very dependent upon the local American Indians to survive.
- The local Indian chief, Wingina, did not trust the English and turned hostile.

Checkpoint

Strengthen

S1 Give two reasons why the English wanted a colony in Virginia.

S2 Give two reasons why Walter Raleigh was important in setting up the colonies.

S3 Give two reasons why the colonies failed.

Challenge

C1 Explain how Raleigh's preparations for the 1585 venture shows he was taking great care to establish a successful colony.

C2 Explain why the type of colonists sent in 1587 was so different from those in 1585.

C3 Explain how the following led to the failures of the 1585 and 1587 colonies:
    a poor luck   b poor judgement.

If you are not confident about any of these questions, form a group with other students, discuss the answers and then record your conclusion. Your teacher can give you some hints.

Recap: Elizabethan society in the Age of Exploration, 1558–88

Recall quiz

1 What were the two main types of school in Elizabethan times?

2 How did literacy rates change in Elizabethan England?

3 What two key developments were there in theatre during Elizabethan times?

4 Give three reasons for increasing poverty in Elizabethan England.

5 What three Acts of Parliament were passed to tackle poverty in Elizabethan England?

6 Give two important changes in the treatment of the poor in Elizabethan England.

7 Give three technological developments that improved Elizabethan sea voyages.

8 Give two causes and two consequences of Drake's circumnavigation of the globe.

9 Give three reasons why settling in Virginia was so important to the English.

10 Give three reasons why England's attempts to colonise Virginia failed.

Exam-style question, Section B

Explain why the attempt to colonise Virginia in 1585–86 was a failure.

You may use the following in your answer:

- the colonists
- Wingina.

You must also use information of your own. **12 marks**

Exam tip

Organise your information before you answer. You have been given two prompts for reasons that you can write about. Choose what other reason(s) you want to include before you begin writing.

Activities

1 Use the table to help remind you of the difference in the two voyages to Virginia during the late 1580s. Do you think any lessons were learned by the 1585–86 failure to colonise Virginia? List as many as you can think of.

When	1585–1586	1587–1590
Who	c 100 male settlers; a mix of landowners, artisans, soldiers and farmers	c 150 settlers, 17 women – two pregnant; many came from the London poor
Fate	Many could not cope with the hardship; relations with the Native Americans failed and Lane abandoned colony; many died from hunger, illness or drowned on the voyage home	117 left in Virginia in August 1587; English ships on a supply mission three years later found the colony abandoned; all the colonists had disappeared

2 To what extent was the failure of the 1585 attempt at colonisation Walter Raleigh's fault? Work in fours. One pair must prepare a case for the prosecution, the other, a case for the defence. Present this to the class, who will be the jury.

3 As you listen to the case for and against Raleigh, make a note of the most convincing evidence. Once this is done, decide whether he was to blame or not. Write up your own, individual verdict in 150–200 words. Your verdict must include factual evidence.

Writing historically: writing cohesively

When you explain events and their consequences, you need to make your explanation as clear and succinct as possible.

Learning outcomes

By the end of this lesson, you will understand how to:

- use pronouns to refer back to ideas earlier in your writing
- use sentence structures to help you refer back to ideas earlier in your writing clearly and economically.

Definition

Pronoun: a word that can stand in for, and refer back to, a noun, e.g. 'he', 'she', 'this', 'that', etc.

How can I refer back to earlier ideas as clearly as possible?

Look at the beginning of a response to this exam-style question below:

> 'The main reason that voyages of exploration were undertaken during Elizabeth I's reign was to increase England's wealth'. How far do you agree?   **(16 marks)**

> *Before Elizabeth encouraged voyages of exploration, Spain controlled much of the New World and was very wealthy. This was a major factor in Elizabeth's desire to discover and claim new land outside of England.*

1. In the second sentence, the **pronoun** 'this' refers back to the first sentence. What could it refer back to?

   a. Spain's wealth   **b.** Spain's control of   **c.** Elizabeth encouraging   **d.** it's not clear – it could be
   the New World   voyages of exploration   referring to any or all of them

One way in which you can improve the clarity of your writing is to avoid imprecise pronouns like 'this' and either:

- repeat the idea you are referring back to OR
- replace it with a word or phrase that summarises the idea.

2. Which of these would you choose to replace 'this' with to make these sentences as clear and precise as possible?

   a. Spain's wealth   **b.** Spain   **c.** the New World   **d.** Elizabeth's ideas

> *Before Elizabeth encouraged voyages of exploration, Spain controlled much of the New World and was very wealthy. This was a major factor in Elizabeth's desire to discover and claim new land outside of England.*

3. Now look at some more sentences from the same response. What could you replace 'This' with to make the sentences as clear as possible?

Sir Francis Drake impressed Elizabeth and the rest of the nobility of England when he circumnavigated the globe, brought back lots of treasure and made his investors very rich. This persuaded Elizabeth to knight him on the deck of the Golden Hind.

How can I structure my sentences to make referring back even clearer?

4. Look at the three versions below of sentences written in response to the exam-style question on the previous page:

Version A

Before Elizabeth pledged her support to Dutch Protestants, the Netherlands provided great trade links with England because they exported cloth and were under Spanish control. This was significant because it antagonised Philip of Spain, damaging relations.

The pronoun 'this' is meant to refer back to this phrase – but, because it follows this clause, the writer has added doubt as to whether 'this' refers to the trade links between the Netherlands and England, the exports of cloth or the influence of Spain on the Netherlands.

Version B

The Netherlands provided great trade links with England because they exported cloth and were under Spanish control before Elizabeth pledged her support to Dutch Protestants. This was significant because it antagonised Philip of Spain, damaging relations.

Version C

Before Elizabeth pledged her support to Dutch Protestants, the Netherlands provided great trade links with England because they exported cloth and were under Spanish control. This change in foreign policy was significant because it antagonised Philip of Spain, damaging relations.

Which version is most clearly expressed and therefore easiest to read? Write a sentence or two explaining your ideas, thinking about: the use of the pronoun 'this', the position of the idea it refers back to and the use of a word or phrase that summarises the idea.

Did you notice?

When you read a text, you usually assume that the pronoun 'this' refers back to the piece of information that you have just read – not the one before that, or the one, two, or three sentences ago.

5. Why are these sentences below unclear and difficult to make sense of?

Philip began plans to invade England. After Elizabeth supported the Dutch Protestants and Drake's voyages in the Pacific, she knighted him on the deck of the Golden Hind. This greatly antagonised Philip.

Improving an answer

6. Experiment with two or three different ways of rearranging and / or rewriting these sentence fragments below to create sentences that explain as clearly as possible why Philip wanted to invade England.

[1] Dutch Protestants rebelled [2] with Elizabeth's help [3] because she didn't want to lose her only Protestant allies in Europe. [4] This resulted in Philip planning the Armada.

Preparing for your GCSE Paper 2 exam

Paper 2 overview

Your Paper 2 is in two sections that examine the Period Study and British Depth Study. They each count for 20% of your History assessment. The questions on Early Elizabethan England are the British Depth Study and are in Section B of the exam paper. You should save just over half the time allowed for Paper 2 to write your answers to Section B. This will give you a few moments for checking your answers at the end.

History Paper 2	Period Study and British Depth Study			Time 1 hour 45 mins
Section A	Period Study	Answer 3 questions	32 marks	50 mins
Section B	Tudor Depth Option B4	Answer 3 questions	32 marks	55 mins

British Depth Option B4 Early Elizabethan England, 1558–88

You will answer Question 5, which is in three parts:

(a) Describe two features of... (4 marks)

You are given a few lines to write about each feature. Allow five minutes to write your answer. It is only worth four marks, so keep the answer brief and not try to add more information on extra lines.

(b) Explain why... (12 marks)

This question asks you to explain the reasons why something happened. Allow 20 minutes to write your answer. You are given two stimulus (information) points as prompts to help you. You do not have to use the prompts and you will not lose marks by leaving them out. Always remember to add in a new point of your own as well. Higher marks are gained by adding in a point extra to the prompts. You will be given at least two pages in the answer booklet for your answer. This does not mean you should try to fill all the space. The front page of the exam paper tells you 'there may be more space than you need'. Aim to give at least three explained reasons.

(c) (i) OR (ii) How far do you agree? (16 marks)

This question is worth half your marks for the whole of the Depth Study. Make sure you have kept 30 minutes to answer it. You have a choice of statements: (i) or (ii). Before you decide, be clear what the statement is about: what 'concept' it is about and what topic information you will need to respond to it. You will have prompts to help, as for part (b).

The statement can be about the concepts of: cause, significance, consequence, change, continuity, similarity or difference. It is a good idea during revision to practise identifying the concept focus of statements. You could do this with everyday examples and test one another: *the bus was late because it broke down* = statement about cause; *the bus broke down as a result of poor maintenance* = statement about consequence; *the bus service has improved recently* = statement about change.

You must make a judgement on **how far you agree** and you should think about **both** sides of the argument. Plan your answer before you begin to write and put your answer points in two columns: For and Against. You should consider at least three points. Think about it as if you were putting weight on each side to decide what your judgement is going to be for the conclusion. That way your whole answer hangs together – it is coherent. Be clear about your reasons (your criteria) for your judgement – for example why one cause is more important than another. Did it perhaps set others in motion? You must **explain** your answer.

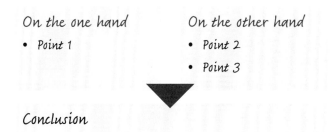

On the one hand
- Point 1

On the other hand
- Point 2
- Point 3

Conclusion

Paper 2, Question 5a

Describe **two** features of Mary, Queen of Scots', threat to Elizabeth I. (**4 marks**)

Exam tip

Keep your answer brief. Two points with some extra information about each feature is all you need.

Average answer

6th

Some people said that Mary, Queen of Scots, had a stronger claim to the English throne than Elizabeth I.

Some Catholics plotted to put Mary, Queen of Scots, on the throne.

The answer identifies two features, but there is no supporting information.

Verdict

This is an average answer because two valid features are given, but there is no supporting information.

Use the feedback to rewrite this answer, making as many improvements as you can.

Strong answer

10th

According to contemporaries, Mary, Queen of Scots, had a stronger claim to the English throne than Elizabeth I. Some Catholics thought that Elizabeth was illegitimate and should not be queen of England.

There were several Roman Catholic plots to put Mary, Queen of Scots, on the throne. The Ridolfi plot of 1571 was organised by an Italian Catholic banker with support from the pope.

The answer has identified two features. It describes what some Catholics thought of Elizabeth I's claim. It also gives an example of a plot that shows that other countries were involved, reinforcing the level of threat

Verdict

This is a strong answer because it gives two clear features of Mary, Queen of Scots' threat to Elizabeth I and gives extra detail to make the descriptions more precise.

Paper 2, Question 5b

Explain **why** Philip II launched the Armada against England in 1588.

You may use the following in your answer:

- England's involvement in the Netherlands
- Drake's attacks on Spain's colonies in America.

You **must** also use information of your own. **(12 marks)**

Exam tip

Don't tell the story of the events. Focus on explaining 'why'. Aim to give at least three reasons.

Average answer

Philip II was the king of Spain. He wanted to marry Elizabeth when she first became queen, but she refused. She did not want to get married because she would be expected to obey her husband.

The Treaty of Nonsuch said England would finance an army of 7,400 troops to help the Dutch rebels. Elizabeth chose Robert Dudley to lead the army. Philip II thought the English should stay out of the Netherlands as they belonged to Spain. This treaty would have made Philip want to attack England.

Drake had been attacking Spain's colonies in America. It is thought that Philip II decided to attack England after raids in 1585. Drake made lots of money raiding Spanish ships and ports and Elizabeth supported him.

Philip II did not like Protestantism. He had sent a big army to the Netherlands in 1567 to get rid of it there. Since then, Elizabeth had helped anyone who was prepared to fight against the Spanish. She let English ships attack Spanish ships. Also, Philip was involved in lots of plots against Elizabeth. By the time Philip II launched the Armada, relations with England had been bad for a long time. However, the Armada was defeated by the English and destroyed as the Spanish ships sailed home around Scotland.

The information here is accurate, but it is not very relevant. It is describing background information and is not a reason for him to launch the Armada.

This focuses on events that led more directly to the Armada. It is still very descriptive, though the last sentence links back to the question focus clearly.

Although there is a reason why Philip II launched the Armada, it needs to be linked to the question and developed. However, the point about timing is a good one.

A reason for Philip II to launch the Armada is hinted at, but it is not very clear. The conclusion is more focused on telling the story of what happened.

Verdict

This is an average answer because:

- information is accurate, showing some knowledge and understanding of the period, and adds a point additional to the stimulus (so it is not a weak answer)
- it does not analyse causes enough to be a strong answer
- there is some development of material, but the line of reasoning is not clear.

Use the feedback to rewrite this answer, making as many improvements as you can.

Paper 2, Question 5b

Explain **why** Philip II launched the Armada against England in 1588. **(12 marks)**

Strong answer

Although Philip II launched the Armada in 1588, he decided to attack England in 1585 after years of worsening relations with Elizabeth I. Both English involvement in the Netherlands (the Treaty of Nonsuch) and raids on Spanish colonies were important reasons. However, Philip II's religious beliefs also explain his decision.

The Treaty of Nonsuch was signed by Elizabeth I in 1585. It promised to finance 7,400 soldiers to help the Dutch Protestant rebels fight the Spanish. Elizabeth sent an army to the Netherlands under the Earl of Leicester. The Netherlands belonged to Spain so this meant that England and Spain were effectively at war. Philip II was even angrier when Leicester accepted the title of Governor General of the Netherlands. Philip II saw it as Elizabeth I trying to depose him. This was unacceptable and he could not ignore it. So the Treaty of Nonsuch was important in contributing to his decision to attack England.

Elizabeth I also sent Drake to raid Spain and Spanish settlements in America in October 1585. These were part of a series of English raids against Spain. Earlier, in 1577, when Drake began his circumnavigation of the globe, Elizabeth I ordered him to attack Spanish settlements. When Drake returned, she knighted him, but Philip II saw Drake as a pirate. It was after the 1585 raids that Philip II told the pope he intended to invade England. Drake's raids triggered Philip II's decision.

Philip II's religious beliefs did not directly lead to the Armada, but were important. The pope wanted Catholics to overthrow Elizabeth I and replace her with Mary, Queen of Scots. When Philip decided to invade England in 1585, Mary was still alive. In 1586, he supported the Babington plot to put her on the throne. After Mary was executed, the Armada was even more important if Elizabeth was to be overthrown. Philip II's religious beliefs also link to the Netherlands. He wanted to crush Protestantism there. Elizabeth I feared he would turn his army against England and so supported Dutch Protestant rebels.

It was Drake's raids in 1585 that triggered Philip II's decision to launch the Armada, especially because they followed the Treaty of Nonsuch. However, there had been a long-term build-up of tensions and Philip II had become increasingly angry at Elizabeth I because of his strong Catholic beliefs.

The wording of the question has been used and Philip II is the focus. This will help focus the answer that follows. Another cause is also identified, not covered by the stimulus bullets.

Here, there is some well-chosen historical evidence that explains why the Treaty helped lead Philip II to attack England.

Knowledge and understanding of historical events is precise and accurate. This answer shows how events combined to lead to Philip II's decision to invade England.

This points out that religious beliefs linked to the conflict between Spain and England in the Netherlands.

This is quite a brief conclusion but it answers the question directly and shows that Philip II's decision to launch the Armada was the result of a combination of causes.

Verdict

This is a strong answer because:

- the answer is well planned and structured, while the question is focused on throughout
- historical evidence is precise and has been carefully selected to support the points made
- a clear line of reasoning how cause and events combined to lead to the launch of the Armada.

Paper 2, Question 5c

Population growth was the main reason why vagabondage increased in Elizabethan England.

How far do you agree? Explain your answer.

You may use the following in your answer:

- sheep farming
- rising prices.

You must also use information of your own. **(16 marks)**

Exam tip

Consider points 'For' and 'Against' the statement and make a judgement. Be clear about your reasons for agreeing or disagreeing.

Average answer

Vagabonds were homeless people who wandered the country. As the population of England grew, so did the number of vagabonds. More people needed bread and this increased prices but some people couldn't afford to buy enough to eat. More people needed somewhere to live. Rents also went up, causing homelessness. People left their villages to look for work and a better life in the towns. Towns like London had tightly packed shacks outside the city walls where homeless people lived and this caused crime, making things worse.

> This introduces the different threads of this argument clearly, and is supported by specific information.

The woollen cloth trade was very important to England. So much wool was needed that landowners decided to turn to sheep farming. Because they didn't need so many labourers, unemployment increased. New farming methods is another reason why there weren't lots of jobs in the countryside and why people became vagabonds. Anyone guilty of being a vagabond faced harsh punishments like whipping and some could even be executed. This shows vagabondage was serious.

> This needs to focus on explaining the impact of sheep farming in more detail: for example, using specialist terms like 'enclosure' would help to strengthen the reasoning.

Some people were poor because they could not work. They were too old, too sick or disabled. Lots of children were poor, especially if they did not have a father. Women were paid less than men, making them very poor if they didn't have a husband. When there was unemployment, people didn't get paid at all. Unemployment happened when trade was bad and it made vagabondage worse.

> A judgement is given but how it links to population growth or other factors is not clear.

The main reason there was so much vagabondage in Elizabethan England was because the population grew so fast.

Verdict

This is an average answer because:

- it shows some knowledge and understanding of the issue and it adds an additional point to the stimulus (so it is not a weak answer)
- it does not analyse factors enough or provide enough specific examples to support points
- it does not explain criteria for judgement clearly enough to be a strong answer.

Use the feedback to rewrite this answer, making as many improvements as you can.

Paper 2, Question 5c

Population growth was the main reason why vagabondage increased in Elizabethan England.

How far do you agree? Explain your answer. **(16 marks)**

Strong answer

Vagabonds were poverty-stricken, homeless people who did not have anywhere permanent to live. They wandered the country hoping to find work, begging or stealing. Their numbers increased as the population of England was growing fast, which led to rising prices. However, there were other changes, like new ways of farming and enclosure, which added to the number of vagabonds.

Population growth was the underlying cause of rising vagabondage. It led to increases in demand for food, land and jobs, which caused rising prices and rents and falling wages. Wages fell because there were more people needing work and so labour became cheaper. Some employers cut wages because, even if they did, there were lots of people who would still take the jobs. When trade was bad, unemployment made conditions worse, especially in towns. The population grew much faster than food production. This led to higher prices for grain especially, and as much as 80% of poor people's income was spent on bread. The demand for land grew with the population, too, and so rents rose. This forced people off the land, increasing poverty and vagabondage further. As a result, more people fell into poverty and became homeless.

Sheep farming caused rural unemployment too. Woollen cloth accounted for over 80% of England's exports, making sheep farming highly profitable. Landowners therefore turned arable land into pasture. Sir Thomas Smith wrote a pamphlet in the 1560s blaming landowners for causing vagabondage. Flocks of sheep did not need as much labour as crops did, creating more rural unemployment. With no other work, many were forced to become vagabonds in the hope of finding jobs elsewhere.

Periods of economic recession also caused unemployment. [Answer exemplifies the problems resulting from the trade embargo with the Netherlands, noting that this particularly affected the cloth trade – a key part of the economy on which a huge number of livelihoods depended].

All three factors are important causes for increases in poverty and vagabondage. However, the root and most important cause was the rise in population. It caused lower wages and rising food prices and rents. As a result, there was a rise in vagabondage as people left the countryside, which made problems faced in towns even worse.

The introduction explains what vagabonds were. It also outlines key reasons for this. As it is linked to other factors, its importance is clear.

References to vagabonds, new methods of farming and enclosure shows a good understanding of the period.

Clear focus on the stated factor. It also links it to inflation, showing how the two factors interacted to increase vagabondage.

Well written and shows good knowledge and understanding of the period by referring to how unemployment and poverty had different causes in the countryside. Avoiding generalisations could strengthen it as not all landowners turned land into pasture.

A strong conclusion with a judgement using criteria to show the increase in vagabondage (root cause, key to inflation, enclosure, rural depopulation).

Verdict

This is a strong answer because:

- information is wide-ranging and precise
- factors are analysed and their importance is evaluated
- the line of reasoning is coherent and the judgement is appropriately justified with clear criteria.

Answers to Elizabeth Recap Questions

Chapter 1

1 Made up of 19 leading courtiers, advisers, nobles and government officials chosen by the monarch; met at least three times a week; presided over by monarch

2 The Act of Uniformity, the Act of Supremacy and the Royal Injunctions

3 Answers could include: fines; oath of supremacy; visitations; clergy who did not agree risked losing their positions; preaching licences; Ecclesiastical High Commission

4 The north and west of England

5 Answers could include: 400 clergy losing their positions; many areas in England were still Catholic, e.g. Lancashire; Vestment Controversy; Crucifix controversy

6 1566

7 The Treaty of Edinburgh; to establish a Protestant government in Scotland

8 Her husband, Henry Stuart, Lord Darnley

9 Answers could include: Mary, Queen of Scots' claim to throne could be stronger; English Catholics might support Mary, Queen of Scots; 1569 plot against Elizabeth I involving Mary, Queen of Scots

10 The Duke of Norfolk

Chapter 2

1 Revolt of the Northern Earls 1569; Ridolfi plot 1571; Throckmorton plot 1583; Babington plot 1586

2 Answers could include: religion – earls were Catholic; loss of influence at court; desire to replace Elizabeth I with the Catholic Mary, Queen of Scots; Elizabeth I refused to name an heir or to marry

3 Answers could include: it encouraged Catholics to overthrow Elizabeth; it said Catholics no longer had to obey Elizabeth; it encouraged plots (e.g. the Ridolfi plot); it meant Elizabeth I could no longer be sure of her Catholic subjects' loyalty

4 A Catholic priest held in the Tower of London who offered to spy for Walsingham

5 In the event of Elizabeth I's assassination Mary, Queen of Scots, barred from succession; action could only be taken against Mary, Queen of Scots, or anyone else benefitting from Elizabeth's death, after a proper investigation and trial

6 It was a source of wealth (trade in tobacco, sugar cane, silver)

7 1577–1580

8 Answers could include: funding the Dutch rebels; sending mercenaries to the Netherlands; raiding Spain's settlements in the New World, disrupting the flow of silver to Spain

9 8 August 1588

10 Answers could include: Spain's provisions ran out; superior English ships and firepower; problems of communication between Medina-Sidonia and Parma; Parma was not ready or able to help engage the English; Battle of Gravelines; luck – bad weather around British coastline

Chapter 3

1 Petty and grammar

2 Literacy rates for men went up from 20% to 30%; there was no change for women

3 First purpose-built theatres; new, secular plays / banning of mystery plays

4 Answers could include: population growth; unemployment / economic recession; rising prices / wages not rising as fast; enclosure – although this last one is debatable

5 1563 Statute of Artificers; 1572 Vagabonds Act; 1576 Poor Relief Act

6 Answers could include: unemployment was recognised as a genuine cause of poverty; national poor relief; helping able bodied poor to find work / make things to sell

7 Answers could include: galleons could store more provisions; Harriot's improved method of navigation using the Sun; Mercator maps; more stable ships; more masts and sails

8 Answers could include: Causes – revenge on Spain, attacking Spanish colonies, profit; Consequences – Spain angered, Drake knighted, Nova Albion founded, England established as great sea-faring nation, huge personal wealth for Drake

9 Answers could include: base from which to attack Spanish colonies in the New World; development of English colonies for trade and wealth; New World could provide goods that previously came from Mediterranean, which was often dangerous for traders; prevent Spanish domination of New World

10 Answers could include: colonists arrived too late to plant crops; supplies being ruined; inexperienced colonists; inexperience; American Indians' hostility; colonists not co-operating with each other

Index

Key terms are capitalized initially, in bold type with an asterisk.
Headings for topic booklets are shown in italics.

A

Abdicate*,	33
Acts of Parliament	
Act for the Preservation of the Queen's Safety,	47
Act of Supremacy,	21
Act of Uniformity,	21, 22
poor laws,	81, 82
Vagabonds Act,	82
Agents provocateurs,	48
Alba, Duke of,	29–30, 54
Alençon, Duke of,	54, 56, 57
Algonquian people,	92
Altars*,	21, 23
American colonies,	40, 51, 52, 53, 84, 88, 89
animals,	74, 78–79
Antwerp,	51, 55
Apprentice*,	71
Arable farming*,	79
Armada, Spanish,	60–64
Astrolabe*,	85
Autonomy*,	54

B

Babington plot,	46–47
baiting and cock-fighting,	74
Barter*,	91
Battle of Gravelines,	62–63
Bible, Elizabeth I's,	18
Boleyn, Anne (queen of Henry VIII),	13, 15
Bothwell, Earl of,	33

C

Calais,	16, 28–29, 62
Casimir, John,	56
Catholicism,	13, 27–29, 45–46, 61, 74–75
see also Protestanticism; religious settlement	
Cecil, Sir William,	11, 27, 33, 42, 45
children's education,	69–72
Church courts,	24
Church of England,	13, 24–25, 69
Cipher*,	48
Circumnavigate*,	53
circumnavigation,	88–89
Clergy*,	19, 23, 26–27
cloth trade,	78, 84
cock-fighting and baiting,	74
coinage,	16
Colonies*,	88
colonisation attempts,	91–99
Conspiracy*,	43
Council of the North,	45
Counter-Reformation,	27
Courtiers*,	10
craftsmen,	9, 71, 74
Crown*,	11
crucifixes,	26

D

dancing and music,	75
Darnley, Lord,	33
Diocese*,	20
discipline, in schools,	71
Divine right*,	11
Drake, Sir Francis,	40, 50, 52–53, 60, 88–89
Dutch Revolt,	29–30, 41
see also Netherlands, Spanish	

E

Ecclesiastical*,	21
Economic recession*,	80
economy see trade	
education,	69–72
Elizabeth I, Queen, character and portrait,	14–15, 63
enclosures,	78–80
Europe,	28, 53–54
exam preparation,	102–107
Excommunicated*,	29
see also **Papal bull***	
Expeditionary force*,	55
exploration, voyages of,	84–99
Extraordinary taxation*,	10, 11

F

family tree, royal,	17
farmers,	9, 71, 74
farming practices,	78–80
finances,	15–16
Fireships*,	62, 63
food,	78
Foreign policy*,	51
Forster family,	42
France	
foreign policy towards,	14, 28–29, 54, 56, 57
as threat,	16, 29, 32

G

galleons,	61–62, 87
gender,	13–14, 69, 71, 72, 77
Genoese Loan,	30
gentry,	9
German states*,	20
Gilbert, Sir Humfrey,	89
girls, education of,	69, 71
Globe theatre,	75
Golden Hind,	88, 89
government, Elizabethan,	10, 11–12, 47, 48
see also Acts of Parliament	
grammar schools,	69–71
Grenville, Richard,	94
Guise family,	16, 32, 41, 46

H

Hanged, drawn and quartered*,	46
Harriot, Thomas,	92, 94, 97
Hawkins, John,	84, 88
Henry VIII,	13
Heretics*,	27
Holy Communion*,	19
Holy Roman Empire*,	28
humanists,	69

I

Ingram, Davy,	89
Intermediary*,	19
Ipswich,	83

J

James VI, King of Scotland,	59
justice,	10, 15, 24
see also laws	

L

labourers,	9, 72, 74
landownership,	9, 15, 78–80
Lane, Ralph,	94
Last Supper*,	19
latitude and longitude,	86
laws,	46, 81–82
legitimacy,	13
Leicester, Earl of,	36, 42, 43, 59–60
Leicester's Men (theatre company),	75
leisure,	73–75
literature,	74–75
London,	77, 83
longitude and latitude,	86
Lords Lieutenant,	10

M

Manteo,	92, 97
maps,	85–86
marriage, and Elizabeth I,	13–14, 54
Martyr*,	27
Mary, Queen of Scots	
claim to throne,	16, 17, 30, 32, 42–43
plots, and execution,	41–47
scandal and captivity in England,	33–36
Mary I, Queen,	14
Mass*,	18
Medina-Sidonia,	62
Mercator map,	86
Mercenary*,	56
merchants,	9, 51, 71
Militia*,	10
monarch, and Parliament,	11–12
money,	16
Monopoly*,	88
music and dancing,	75
mystery plays,	74–75

N

Native Americans, 89, 91–92, 97
navigation equipment, 85–86
navy, English, 61–62, 64
Netherlands, Spanish
    Dutch Revolt and policy in, 29–30, 41, 45, 50, 54–57
    intervention in, 59–60
Neville family, 45
New World*, 51, 52, 53
    see also American colonies
nobility
    children's education, 69, 72
    and leisure, 73–74
    Revolt of the Northern Earls, 27–28, 30, 36, 41–45
    in society and government, 9, 10
Norfolk, Duke of, 36, 42, 43, 45
North America, expedition to, 91–99
northern England, Catholicism in, 20, 27–28, 41, 45
Northumberland, Earl of, 27, 28, 42, 44
    see also Percy family
North-West Passage, 84
Norwich, 77
Nottingham, Earl of, 63
Nova Albion, 89

P

Pacification of Ghent, 55
Papacy*, 27
    see also popes
Papal bull*, 44–45
Parker, Matthew, archbishop of Canterbury, 27
Parliament, 10, 11–12
    see also Acts of Parliament
Parma, Duke of, 56, 60, 61, 62
Patron*, 11, 53
Percy family, 42, 45
Petty schools, 71
Philip II, King of Spain, 14, 29, 30, 41, 52, 89
    Armada plan, 61–64
Pilgrimage*, 22
Pilkington, James (archbishop of Durham), 42
Pius VI, Pope, 45
plays, religious and secular, 74–75
plots and revolts, 27–28, 30, 36, 41–48
poor, the, 72, 77–83
poor laws, 81, 82
popes, 27, 29, 44–45, 46, 61
population growth, 77
Portugal, 57, 61
prices and wages, 78
priests and priest holes, 26–27, 46, 48

printing, 86
Privateer*, 51, 52
Privy Council, 10, 57
pronouns and synonyms, 100–101
Propaganda*, 63
Protestanticism, 16, 18–19, 28–29, 53–54, 57, 69
    see also Catholicism; religious settlement
punishment, 71, 81–83
Puritans, 21, 22, 26

Q

Quadrant*, 85
Queen regnant*, 14

R

Raleigh, Walter, 91–94, 95
rebellions see plots and revolts
Recusants*, 24, 47
Reformation*, 18, 19
religious divisions and rivalry, 19–21, 53–54
religious settlement, 18–31
Revolt of the Northern Earls, 27–28, 30, 36, 41–45
Rhetoric*, 72
Ridolfi plot, 45
Roanoke Island, 94–98
Roman Catholic*, 13, 18–19
Rome*, 29
Royal Injunctions, 21, 22
Royal prerogative*, 12, 43
Royal Supremacy*, 22
Rural depopulation*, 79

S

Sacking*, 55
Sacraments*, 19
Saints*, 22
schools, 69–72
Scotland, 16, 28, 29, 32, 33
Secretary of States, 11, 48
sentence structuring, 38–39, 100–101
settlement, religious, 18–31
sheep farming, 78–79
    see also wool trade
ships, 61–62, 85–87, 94
slavery, 84
Social mobility*, 69
society, Elizabethan, 9
Spain
    colonies, 95
    foreign policy and relations with, 14, 41, 50–58, 88, 89
    as threat, 16, 29–30, 41, 43, 45, 47–48
    war with, 59–64, 84

Spanish Fury, 55
Spanish Inquisition*, 29–30
sport, 73–74
Stanley, Sir William, 59
Statute of Artificers, 82
Subsistence farming*, 79
Succession*, 12, 42–43
synonyms and pronouns, 100–101

T

taxes, 10, 11, 15, 16
theatres, 74–75
Throckmorton plot, 46
Timeline: Elizabethan England, 6–7
tobacco, 84, 95
towns, 9, 80
trade, 51, 80, 84, 95
Trade embargo*, 29
transubstantiation, 22
treason, 45
Treaty of Berwick, 59
Treaty of Joinville, 57
Treaty of Nonsuch, 59
Triangular Trade, 84

U

unemployment, 80, 82
universities, 72
urban poor, 80

V

Vagabonds* (vagrants), 80, 81–83
vestment controversy, 26–27
Virginia, expedition to, 91–99
visitations, 25

W

wages and prices, 78
Walsingham, Sir Francis, 46, 47, 48
Wanchese, 92
Westmorland, Earl of, 27, 28, 42
    see also Neville family
White, John, 97–98
William of Orange, 57
Wingina, Chief, 97
women/girls, 13–14, 69, 71, 72, 77
wool trade, 78, 84
working people, and leisure, 74
writing historically: sentences, 38–39, 66–67

Y

yeoman, 9

Acknowledgements

The publisher would like to thank the following for their kind permission to reproduce their photographs: (Key: b-bottom; c-centre; l-left; r-right; t-top)

Bridgeman Art Library Ltd: Bibliotheque Nationale, Paris, France 55, Bridgeman / The Stapleton Collection / Private Collection 26, Burghley House Collection, Lincolnshire, UK 11, Hardwick Hall, Derbyshire, UK / National Trust Photographic Library 7c, 34, Hugo Maertens 57tr, National Gallery, London, UK 15, Parham House, West Sussex, UK / Photo © Mark Fiennes 59, Private Collection 6, 7tr, 8, 30, 63, 68, 73, 75, 86, Scottish National Portrait Gallery, Edinburgh, Scotland 40, 47; **Getty Images:** Heritage Images / Fine Art Images 57tc; **Mary Evans Picture Library:** 70; **The Art Archive:** 12; **TopFoto:** Bridgeman Images 18, British Library Board 97, Fotomas 81, World History Archive 85

Cover images: *Front:* **Bridgeman Art Library Ltd:** National Portrait Gallery, London, UK

All other images © Pearson Education

We are grateful to the following for permission to reproduce copyright material:

Extract on page 14, Interpretation 1, from *Elizabeth I* 1 edition, Routledge (Haigh,Christopher) p.16; Extract on page 22, Interpretation 1, from *Access to History: Change and Protest 1536–88: Mid-Tudor Crises?*, 4th Revised edition, Hodder Education (Heard,N Turvey,R) p.112, reproduced with permission of Hodder Education; Extract on page 27, Interpretation 1, from *The Reign of Elizabeth: England 1558–1603*, Reprint edition, Hodder Education (Mervyn,B) p.129, reproduced with permission of Hodder Education; Extract on page 34, Interpretation 1, from *New World, Lost Worlds: The Rule of the Tudors 1485–1603*, Viking Books (Brigden, S 2001) p.227, copyright © Susan Bridgen, 2000; Extract on page 52, Interpretation 1, from *The Great Expedition: Sir Francis Drake on the Spanish Main – 1585–86*, Osprey Publishing (Konstam, A), © Osprey Publishing, part of Bloomsbury; Extract on page 57, Interpretation 2, from *Elizabeth I: Meeting the Challenge, England 1541–1603*, Hodder Education (Warren, W), reproduced with permission of Hodder Education; Extract on page 63, Interpretation 1, from Why the Spanish Armada Failed, *History Today* 38 (Parker, G), with permission from History Today; Extract on page 76, Interpretation 1, from *The Elizabethans* Arrow Books (Wilson AN) p.265, published by Hutchinson, reproduced by permission of The Random House Group Ltd; Extract on page 79, Interpretation 1, from *Time Travellers Guide to Elizabethan England*, Vintage (Mortimer,I) p.22, published by Bodley Head, reproduced by permission of The Random House Group Ltd, copyright © 2012 by Forrester Mortimer Ltd, also used by permission of Viking Books, an imprint of Penguin Publishing Group, a division of Penguin Random House LLC; Extract on page 88, Interpretation 1, from Drake's Voyage Around the World, *History Today* 17 (Hamshere, C.E), with permission from History Today; Extract on page 95, Interpretation 1, from *Roanoke: The Abandoned Colony*, Rowman and Littlefield (Kupperman,KO), reproduced with permission of Rowman & Littlefield in the format Republish in a book via Copyright Clearance Center; Extract on page 96, Interpretation 2, from *Big Chief Elizabeth* Sceptre (Milton, G), reproduced by permission of Hodder and Stoughton Limited.